HAND-STITCHED
HOME

PROJECTS TO SEW
WITH PENDLETON
& OTHER WOOLS

SUSAN BEAL

The Taunton Press
Inspiration for hands-on living®

To Julie and Michelle, for their friendship and inspiration

The Taunton Press
Inspiration for hands-on living®

The Taunton Press, Inc.,
63 South Main Street, PO Box 5506
Newtown, CT 06470-5506
e-mail: tp@taunton.com

Executive Editor: Shawna Mullen
Editor: Ashley Little
Assistant Editor: Tim Stobierski
Copy Editor: Betty Christiansen
Indexer: Barbara Mortenson
Cover design: Kathie Alexander
Interior design: Kathie Alexander
Layout: Rita Sowins
Illustrator: Alexis Hartman
Art Director: Rosalind Loeb Wanke
Photo Editor: Erin Giunta
Photographers: All photos by Burcu Avsar, except for p. 79 courtesy of Marie Watt and the Denver Museum of Art; p. 156 by Nancy Flynn; and all historical images throughout text courtesy of Pendleton Woolen Mills®
Prop Stylist: Michelle Wong

Library of Congress Cataloging-in-Publication Data

Beal, Susan.
 Hand-stitched home : projects to sew with Pendleton & other wools / author, Susan Beal.
    pages cm
  ISBN 978-1-62113-870-9 (paperback)
1. Sewing. 2. Wool fabrics. 3. House furnishings. 4. Tailoring--Patterns. I. Title. II. Title: Handstitched home.
 TT705.B3185 2014
 646.2--dc23
                            2014016472
Printed in the United States of America
10 9 8 7 6 5 4 3 2 1

Acknowledgments

This book was truly a dream project, and I am so grateful to the many kind and wonderful people who made it possible. Thank you all, more than I can say.

My deepest thanks to everyone at Pendleton Woolen Mills for their generous support, and especially for the beautiful fabrics they shared for the projects. I'm so thankful for the chance to design, sew, write, and research for this book. Thank you to Julie Fisher, Kathy Monaghan, and Robert Christnacht for letting me share my ideas, and to the board of directors and fifth-generation Pendleton President Mort Bishop for their faith in me and in this book.

Thank you so much to Linda Parker and to Kathy for their time and thoughtful attention to my project. Thank you to everyone in fabric design: to Marsha Hahn for her lovely contribution, to Nicole Betz for the fascinating tour, and to Winthur Sempliner for her great stories. I'm so grateful to Ric Drury and Greg Day for providing many fantastic images and articles from Pendleton's history, which brought my research to life. Thank you to historian Richard Hobbs for all his assistance in the vast company archives, where we looked through everything from President Obama's and Walt Disney's personal thank-you notes to Lester Kiser's dyeing notebooks—not to mention the dozens of gorgeous '49er jackets, a personal favorite of mine!

Thank you to everyone at the Woolen Mill Store: Julie, Tawnya, Cally, Stacy, Jessie, Mimi, and Adam for your wonderful help. And Michelle Freedman was an inspiration throughout, from her sewing knowledge to her eye for color and design.

I'm so lucky to have stellar project contributors. Thank you to Diane Gilleland, Amy Alan, Haley Pierson-Cox, Anna Joyce, Sandie Holtman, Amber Corcoran, Stacy Brisbee, Sarai Mitnick, Heather Mann, Michelle Freedman, Meredith Neal, Alexia Marcelle Abegg, Lupine Swanson, and Cally McVay for sharing your beautiful work! Each piece is so wonderful, and I know how much time and care went into each of them.

A huge thank-you to my lovely editor, Shawna Mullen—who has a great Pendleton story of her own—and to Timothy Stobierski and Ashley Little. Thanks to my always-wonderful agent Stacey Glick and longtime illustrator extraordinaire Alexis Hartman. Rosalind Loeb Wanke and Erin Giunta did such a beautiful job with the visuals throughout, while Burcu Avsar, Michelle Wong, and Megan Senior created such gorgeous photographs. It was so much fun to spend a few sunny days on the Spirit Horse Farm in Kent, Connecticut.

Finally, I'm so grateful for the love and support of my family: my daughter, Pearl, who adores the button, scrap, and buckle treasures she always finds at the Woolen Mill Store; my son, Everett, a true fall baby who still loves to cuddle under a cozy wool patchwork blanket; and my husband, Andrew, who always believes in me and just knew this book idea that was so close to my heart would find a home. And it did.

Contents

Introduction

It seems like *everyone* has a Pendleton story. The name resonates with warm associations—a treasured blanket passed down through generations, a favorite vintage coat passed on from father to son, or a classic skirt from mother to daughter.

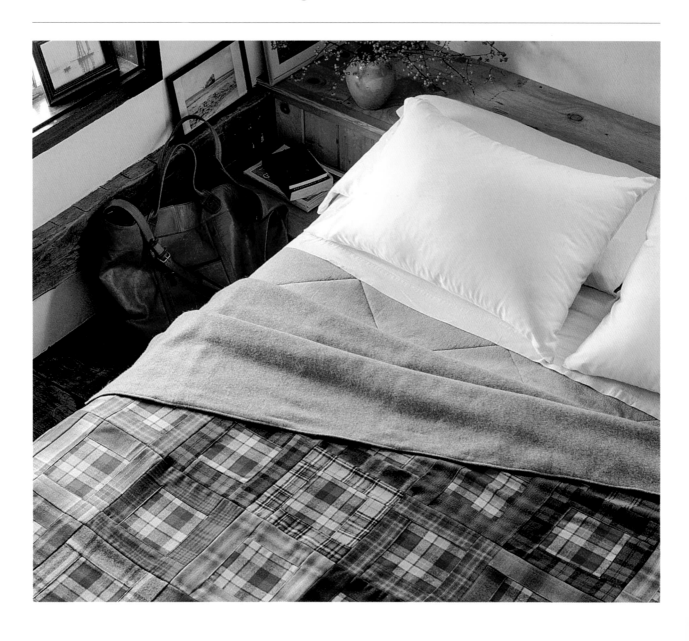

But in addition to Pendleton's renowned blankets and clothing, sewists and designers seek out their fabrics and yarns for making their own beautiful handmade projects. Whether they're buying fabric yardage off the roll or scraps by the pound, crafters all over the country and the world make truly wonderful things with Pendleton fabric. Pendleton's patterns and plaids are instantly recognizable, and the colors, texture, and quality are unmatched for creative possibilities—and wonderful to work with, too.

So whether you've been sewing with wool all your life, or have a very first dream project of your own in mind, I hope this book inspires you. I included some of my own all-time favorite projects—the ones I use in my home every day—and asked 14 of my favorite designers to contribute their ideas, too. I was more and more excited with each project they suggested, and of course, we were all thrilled that Pendleton generously provided their beautiful fabric.

I've shared my techniques on everything from pressing and cutting to binding and topstitching, and my contributors have offered their own invaluable tips on working with leather, matching plaids, and all the other little things that make a handmade sewing project not just beautiful, but special.

The projects in this book were all created with Pendleton wools, but you can substitute with any fabrics that match in weight. To help with substitutions, I've listed the Pendleton wools that were used for each project, followed by their general fabric equivalents, with each project; p. 10 also offers a breakdown of Pendleton fabrics and what you can substitute them with.

One Sheep, Two Sheep … Projects to Sew

Each project in the book is rated for difficulty by the number of sheep—a Pendleton tradition!

 One sheep: beginner-friendly and easy

 Two sheep: a bit more involved

 Three sheep: moderately difficult or includes multiple techniques; perfect for intermediate sewists

 Four sheep: advanced or larger-scale project for experienced sewists

The 27 sewing and quilting projects presented in these pages include everyday essentials like the **Classic Blanket** (p. 70) and stylish **School Days Messenger Bag** (p. 108), along with modern heirlooms like the **Improvisational Patchwork Quilt** (p. 84) and the **Jacquard Cube Ottoman** (p. 64). Try your hand at the smaller projects, and then move up to the larger pillows, blankets, and throws. I hope you enjoy working with the warm and beautiful textures, colors, and designs that wool fabric has to offer.

I also hope you will find inspiration in both the sewing techniques and the many stitching projects in the following chapters. We've also set up a book website with bonus material, more sewing tips, and lots of extras at westcoastcrafty.com—I hope you'll visit there and share your own Pendleton story, too.

Happy sewing!

Susan

1 About Pendleton

The deepest roots and most impressive branches of Pendleton Woolen Mills remain steadfast well into its sixth generation. Pendleton has been weaving beautiful wool fabrics in the Pacific Northwest for more than a century. From the first vividly patterned Indian trade blankets to THE PORTLAND COLLECTION's ultra-modern silhouettes, the company has always offered distinctive and universally appealing quality.

All of *Pendleton's* trade blankets and jacquard, plaid, and solid fabrics are still woven in their own mills in Oregon and Washington. The beautiful Chief Joseph and Harding jacquards so popular in the early days of the company are still in the current line, and Pendleton's remarkable pattern of innovation continues in the early 21st century.

The Arts and Crafts movement, inspired by nature and handcraft, and with a hallmark of fine workmanship, flourished in the early 20th century—particularly in response to the fast pace of modern life, with its humming factories and dirty, crowded cities. Pendleton's early catalogs offered a colorful variety of designs in this style, displayed in an appealing and serene setting; it was said that an Indian trade blanket "replenished the atmosphere with colorful naturalness and a resplendent calm" within a room or a home.

You can visit many of the Pendleton mills in person: The 1912 Washougal mill in Washington, which primarily weaves garment fabrics, and the original Pendleton mill in Eastern Oregon, which weaves blankets, both offer free daily tours throughout the week. The former 1939 Milwaukie Mill (just south of Portland) has been transformed into the retail-only Woolen Mill Store, offering home sewists everything from huge rolls of plaid, solid, and jacquard fabrics by the yard to bins of colorful wool scraps of all shapes and sizes, sold by the pound. Meanwhile, the 1889 Thomas Kay Woolen Mill in Salem is now a museum—the Willamette Heritage Center—open to the public.

For much more on Pendleton's history, see the timeline on p. 144.

Provided courtesy of Pendleton Woolen Mills

Fabric Production:
From Raw Wool to Retail

The first step in the weaving process is the purchase of raw wool. Pendleton wool buyers shop world markets, but most of Pendleton's wool still comes from the United States. Variety, quality, and quantity of wool fibers are essential to produce fine Pendleton woolens.

Pendleton's in-house fabric design department has a beautifully organized archive of thousands of historic fabric swatches on cards, including plaids, solids, and jacquards. Designers can look to vintage collections for new inspiration, perhaps choosing an iconic design and reweaving new fabric samples in a variety of colorways or scales by hand on small looms. From there, colors and details are narrowed down and finalized, and designs are then sent to the two working mills for large-scale production.

Fabric production includes many steps: dyeing, carding, spinning, weaving, and finishing. Dyeing is accomplished by computer-controlled systems that immerse the wool in water and dye, then set the color with heat and flow pressure. The carding process combs and aligns fibers in preparation for spinning. During spinning, strands of fibers are extended and twisted to form yarns. Then, high-speed computerized looms interlace the yarns into woven cloth, whether it's an intricate, graphic jacquard pattern for a cozy blanket, or a crisp menswear plaid flannel. Due to the unique felting property of wool, the woven cloth goes through a fulling process that uses controlled shrinkage to produce a softer, more compact fabric. The material also passes through other finishing procedures, such as washing, shearing, pressing, and napping before production is complete. Near the end of the cycle, blanket fabrics are cut and finished while fashion fabrics are sent to garment plants for apparel production.

These images provided courtesy of Pendleton Woolen Mills.

2 Tools, Materials & Techniques

Having the correct materials and tools on hand is essential before beginning any new project. Let me show you exactly what you need, and need to know, to complete all of the handmade projects in this book.

Tools and Materials

Whether you're a sewing beginner or just new to *sewing with wool,* here are a few of the tools and materials you'll use to sew the projects in this book.

All About Wool

Pendleton wools can be purchased through the Woolen Mill Store in Portland, Oregon, or their online store. You can also use wools of your own choosing for any of the projects in this book. Here's a primer for everything you'll need to know about each type of wool.

Wool Fabrics

These are just a few of the types of wool fabric available—and some of the most useful for home sewing projects of all kinds. You'll find recommendations for which types of wool fabric to use in each project description. The list is arranged from lightest to heaviest weight.

Worsted (4–5.7 oz./yd.): This ultra-light, crisp wool is ideal for linings or for backing heavier quilts. It can also be used for apparel sewing and is very versatile; it tears, sews, pins, and presses beautifully. Worsted wool is generally 58 in. to 60 in. wide.

Shirtweight Flannel (10–12 oz./yd.): Just slightly heavier than worsted, this fabric is supple, is lightweight, and has a wonderful hand. It's often woven in distinctive plaid patterns. You can use it for everything from pillow covers to lining bags and piecing quilt blocks—and, of course, to sew the shirts the flannel was originally created for. Shirtweight flannel is generally 58 in. to 60 in. wide, and some flannels are machine washable.

Merino (16 oz./yd.): A lush lightweight fabric, merino is woven from soft merino wool and is ideal for special gifts like a baby blanket or a luxurious scarf. Merino fabrics can be plaids or solids, and they generally tear and sew quite easily.

Jacquard Wool (16 oz./yd.): This wool is a flexible, midweight, soft but sturdy fabric that's wonderful for many projects. Use it to sew coats, capes, bags, upholstery, and many other designs. The distinctive jacquard pattern is woven in on the loom and often reflects an opposite colorway on the back, which gives lots of design flexibility. This weight and type of fabric can also be found in solid or reversible solid colors, and the fabric tears well. Can be substituted with any midweight wool.

Melton (24 oz./yd.): A dense, napped midweight fabric designed for coats and jackets, melton is also a versatile, sturdy fabric for bags or other projects. This wool is available in solids only and is generally 58 in. to 60 in. wide.

Jacquard Blanket (32 oz./yd.): Like the jacquard wool, this beautifully detailed fabric is also woven on a loom, but its weight, thickness, and warmth are much greater. This fabric is wonderful for binding as a classic blanket, or piecing into a simple quilt design. Can be substituted with any blanket-weight wool. Do not tear blanket-weight fabric; it should be carefully cut with shears or a rotary cutter.

Pendleton Eco-Wise Wool® (18 oz./yd.): A special upholstery-weight fabric in solid colors, much like a heavier flannel, Pendleton Eco-Wise Wool is sustainably sourced and dyed, and can be recycled or even composted. It's approximately 55 in. wide and tears beautifully. It can be substituted with any upholstery-weight wool.

Substituting Wools

While the projects in this book were sewn using a variety of Pendleton wool fabrics, you can also use other vintage or new wool fabrics, if desired. When searching for substitutes, make sure that the substitute fabric is of the same general weight as the wool used in the project, and that the fiber content and overall texture match. See Resources (p. 148) for suggestions on where to buy vintage, new, and scrap Pendleton fabrics.

Wool Binding Fabric

You can buy Pendleton's own 1½-in.-wide wool felt binding by the yard in a huge array of colors, and trim it down to a narrower width if you choose.

Stitching Wool

Hand Stitching

For hand-sewing wool fabrics, I generally recommend using a sharp crewel or embroidery needle. I love to blanket-stitch or embroider with pearl cotton, a soft, thick, beautifully twisted single strand of colorful floss. Many of the projects in this book use DMC® pearl cotton, with the color numbers noted. You can also use a thinner thread or embroidery floss or wool cording. Knot on the wrong side of your fabric, or bury the floss between two layers of fabric if you're using them.

Machine Sewing

Sewing your wool fabric projects with a sewing machine is very easy. I recommend using a sharp machine needle and changing your needle between projects.

I use 100 percent cotton or polyester thread for sewing my wool projects, and I adjust stitch length depending on the weight and number of layers of my fabrics. For worsted or flannels, I use a standard stitch length and increase it for binding a blanket, topstitching or perimeter-stitching multiple layers of wool, and so on. Always test stitch length on scraps before you begin sewing to be sure you are using the appropriate length.

A Look Back: Home Sewing with Pendleton Fabrics

Pendleton began sponsoring the national *Make It Yourself With Wool* contest when it got its start in the late 1940s. To encourage high-quality home sewing and garment care, the company offered free educational brochures and pamphlets like "Pressing Wool" and "Wool Responds Beautifully to Easy Care," published by Emma Rogness of the company's home economics division. Pendleton sent out thousands of these pamphlets to 4-H clubs, schools, and shops (over 80,000 in 1965 alone), and Mrs. Rogness often judged the *Make It Yourself With Wool* sewing entries, awarding prizes like college scholarships and even trips around the world to the winners at the national conventions—including the one held in Oregon to commemorate the state's centennial in 1959. Pendleton fabrics were available in the finest department stores for home sewists to make couture-quality garments, always on trend, just as they are in the Woolen Mill Store today—and Pendleton still sponsors *Make It Yourself With Wool*.

Provided courtesy of Pendleton Woolen Mills

Basic Sewing Tools

To make the projects in this book, you'll need a few basic sewing tools and a few little extras that you might not be familiar with. Here are a few of my recommendations for specific tools to make sure you have everything you need to sew these beautiful wool fabrics.

Iron

You'll need a good-quality steam iron for pressing wool—using a dry iron can scorch or damage fabric. I also like to have a spray bottle of distilled water handy for pressing creases and folds.

Cutting Tools

I use sharp fabric shears to cut wool, or a medium-size or large rotary cutter with a straightedge clear quilting ruler and self-healing cutting mat. You can also tear wool for an astonishingly accurate "cut." (See p. 13 for instructions on tearing.)

Pins

Sharp pins, particularly the oversize ones with larger heads, are easy to spot when pinning fabrics together.

Tracing Paper

Semi-opaque pattern paper (I love the kind with dots to mark inches or other increments) is ideal for tracing patterns and their markings.

Interfacing

I use both double-sided interfacing and adhesive double-sided fabric bonding sheets, such as Phoomph™, for creating interesting three-dimensional projects like the **Nesting Boxes** (p. 32) and **Square Coasters and Trivet** (p. 38). Always test these materials with fabric scraps to see how their weights and adhesives work with your chosen fabrics.

Snaps

Large sew-in snaps or magnetic snaps are both ideal for simple closures on your scarves, bags, or other wool projects—just follow the manufacturer's instructions to add them to your fabric.

Walking Foot

A walking foot can be helpful for feeding thicker projects neatly through your sewing machine.

Zippers

Use metal zippers for larger, sturdier projects like a laptop case or full-size upholstery project, following package directions to insert and sew them.

For pillow covers, a lighter-weight invisible zipper is fine. Be sure to use a special invisible zipper foot, which makes sewing them very easy! You can find instructions for installing an invisible zipper on pp. 20–21.

Pillows

Pillow forms stuffed with batting or down generally come in standard sizes—we used 12-in., 14-in., 18-in., and 20-in. square forms in our projects, plus a 14-in. by 28-in. rectangular bolster.

Techniques

Sewing with Pendleton wool is absolutely wonderful—it presses beautifully, stitches like butter, and will last to become a family heirloom. Here are some basic techniques you'll use to create many of the projects in this book.

Tearing and Cutting Wool

There are two ways you can prep your fabric: tearing or cutting. Believe it or not, you can tear many wools precisely along a grainline much more accurately (and quickly!) than you could possibly cut them straight with scissors or a rotary cutter. However, heavier fabrics are a little more difficult to tear; for those, you'll cut the fabric. Here are instructions for both tearing and cutting:

Tearing

This method feels a little like a leap of faith the first time you try it, but you'll be amazed at the results. Here's how to tear your fabric:

1. Make a small cut through the selvage. Many wool fabrics are woven with a strand of filament at the selvage edge for stability, which doesn't tear as easily.

2. Holding the fabric above and below the small cut, decisively tear the fabric into two pieces. You'll see the tear follow a grainline with perfect accuracy.

3. Continue tearing until you reach the other selvage (or where you want to stop).

4. Cut the second selvage with scissors. Clear away any loose threads.

5. Repeat on either grainline to tear straight lines across your wool fabric.

Cutting

The heaviest blanket fabrics won't tear due to their weave and weight.

Cutting pattern pieces out of wool is very similar to cutting quilting cottons or other fabrics: Pin or weight your pattern pieces down, following a grainline, and carefully cut with sharp fabric scissors or a rotary cutter.

Pressing

Wool fabric loves a steam iron and responds very nicely to careful pressing. Here are a few tips for pressing wool:

- Use a steam iron on a wool setting and test on a scrap of fabric first. I also like to use a small spray bottle of distilled water on stubborn folds or crease marks. The wool will form a beautiful shape when pressed with steam, from crisp folds to smooth curves.

- Use a lightweight pressing cloth over your wool if your test scrap shows any shine or heat evidence. A dry iron can scorch wool, so be careful to always use steam or spray water to keep it from damaging the fibers.

- When pressing seam allowances at the back of your work, move the iron smoothly over the folds. Don't press down too hard, but guide the iron over the fabric fold in the direction you want it to lie flat. Press the back and then the front for neat results.

- When piecing or topstitching continuously at your machine, you may be able to save yourself an extra trip to the ironing board by finger pressing. Finger pressing involves smoothing a fold or double layer to the correct side with your hands before topstitching or adding another patchwork piece there. Always check the back of your work before moving on; you can simply use a seam ripper to carefully open and repair any misfolds, then re-sew.

Piecing

Patchwork

Piecing, or sewing pieces of wool together patchwork-style, is just as easy as sewing more familiar fabrics like quilting cottons. I always recommend a larger seam allowance for wool patchwork, particularly on sturdier or heavier-weight fabrics—½ in. is a good general seam allowance rather than the ¼ in. often called for in cotton patchwork. When piecing wool, you often don't need to backstitch since the seam ends will disappear into another seamline.

To reinforce and accentuate seamlines, topstitch around the piecing, catching a fabric fold underneath. This creates a crisp and smooth line, but also adds stability and smoothness to the layers of fabric. See "Topstitching" (p. 18) for more details.

Log Cabin Piecing

You'll see this simple design in several projects in the book, such as the **Square Coasters and Trivet** on p. 38. Log cabin piecing is simply adding "logs" (strips of fabric) around a central square. Here's how:

1. Cut center squares of one fabric and longer strips of another one. (Each project will give you specific instructions for the size of the squares and strips.)

2. Align the square over the strip, right sides together, with edges matching exactly. Stitch the two fabrics together using a ½-in. seam allowance. Trim the strip at the bottom edge of the center square.

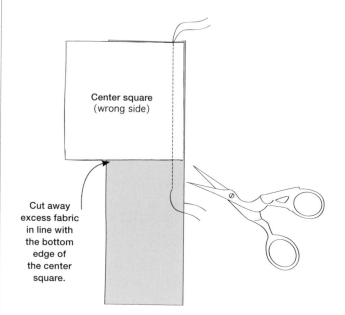

Center square (wrong side)

Cut away excess fabric in line with the bottom edge of the center square.

3. Press or finger-press your seam on the back away from the center square, toward the log.

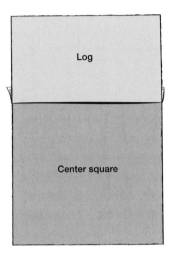

4. Working clockwise, repeat steps 2 and 3, aligning the center square and the first log over the strip and adding the second log the same way you added the first log.

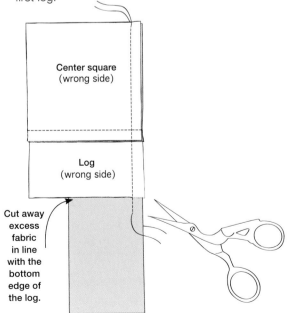

Center square (wrong side)

Log (wrong side)

Cut away excess fabric in line with the bottom edge of the log.

5. You now have two logs around the square.

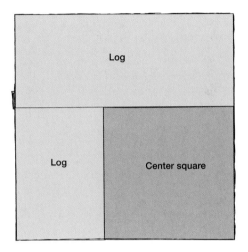

6. Continue to work clockwise, adding a third log.

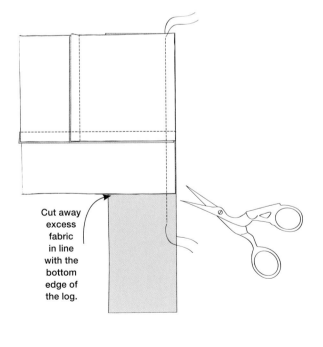

Cut away excess fabric in line with the bottom edge of the log.

7. You will now have three logs around the square.

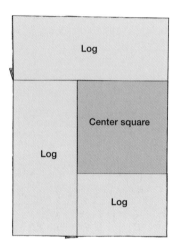

8. Repeat steps 2 and 3 once more, adding a fourth log to the square.

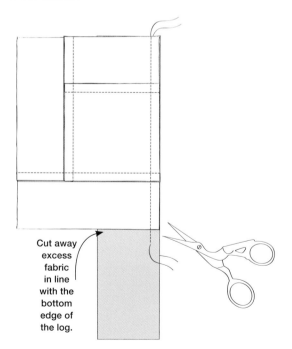

Cut away excess fabric in line with the bottom edge of the log.

9. You now have four logs around the square.

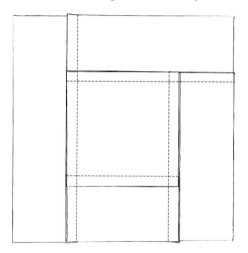

10. Press the back and front of this block with your steam iron. You can quickly join strips if you need longer lengths for finishing blocks. I recommend top-stitching along the seam (p. 18), as shown here.

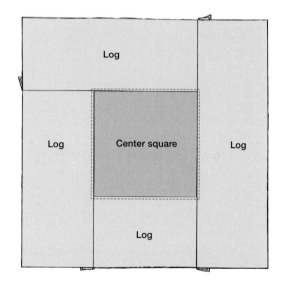

11. Stop here for the **Square Coasters** on p. 40 or **Square-Within-a-Square Plaid Quilt** on p. 80. Add a second ring of logs for the **Square Trivet** on p. 39.

Chain Piecing

Chain piecing is especially handy for larger piecing projects, like a quilt, because it saves a lot of time. Here's how to do it:

1. Cut your center squares and strips, in this case sewing five blocks with the same logs.

2. Align the first square on the strip just as you would for standard log cabin piecing and sew it, but instead of stopping and trimming, simply align a second square just after the first one on the same strip and continue sewing.

3. Add the third, fourth, and fifth squares the same way. Remove the strip from the machine.

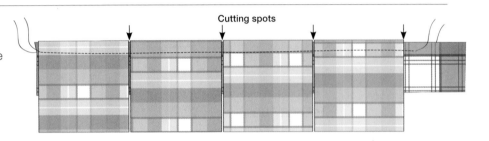

4. Trim each square neatly—each one will have its first log—and press or finger-press the seam away from the center square.

5. Align a center square and the first log pair on the strip of fabric and stitch it down. Working clockwise, add a second pair just after the first. Continue sewing until you have joined all five second logs or until you have reached the end of the strip, whichever comes first.

6. Trim all sections and press or finger-press. Continue chain piecing the same way to add all third and then all fourth logs.

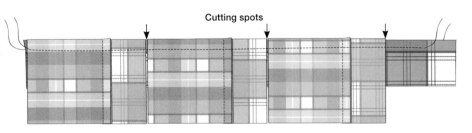

7. Press the backs and fronts of your blocks with your steam iron.

Stitches

You'll use many different types of stitches for the projects in this book. Some are decorative, while others are necessary for the construction of the project. Here are a few of the most common stitches found throughout the book.

Topstitching

After joining wool fabrics into a patchwork or layered design, I recommend topstitching along the seam for both a neat, smooth finish and a decorative element.

To topstitch, simply press your seam to one side and pin or hold it in place. Use a straight stitch to follow the line of the seam, just to one side of it, catching all layers of the fabric with the stitching. You can see stylized examples of this technique in the **Wool Cross Pillows** on p. 60 and the **Square-Within-a-Square Plaid Quilt** on p. 80. You can also see an example of topstitching in the piecing of the **Improvisational Patchwork Quilt** on p. 84.

You can also press your seams open and topstitch on either side of your seam for a parallel row of stitching, as in the **Improvisational Chevron Bolster** on p. 54. Using contrast thread, as Amy Alan did for her **Modern Plant Hanger** on p. 42, can be an eye-catching touch. Topstitching close to an edge is called edgestitching.

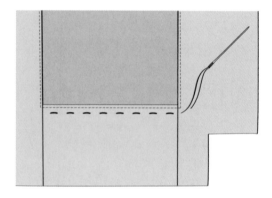

Running Stitch

This simple handstitch couldn't be easier: Just thread a needle, hide your knot on the wrong side of the fabric, and stitch forward, dipping your needle into the fabric and bringing it out to make basic straight-line stitches.

You can use a large, casual version of this stitch to temporarily baste two fabrics together, like the silk lining and wool for the **Fitted Scarf** on p. 116. You can also use neat, organized stitches as decorative elements in projects like the **Leaf Table Runner** on p. 26 and **Square Coasters and Trivet** on p. 38.

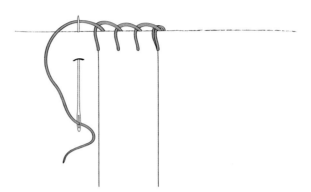

Blanket Stitch

This very useful hand stitch creates a nicely finished handmade edge on a project and neatly joins two layers of fabric together. The blanket stitch is used in projects like the **Men's Scarf** on p. 118 or the **Nesting Boxes** on p. 32. Practice it on scraps first to get the hang of it and choose the scale of your stitches.

Here's how to make a blanket stitch:

1. Thread a crewel needle with a single strand of pearl cotton or yarn. Tie a knot at one end and bury it between the two layers of fabric, bringing the thread from the inside through one fabric.

2. Bring the thread around to the back of the second fabric to create a beginning "anchor" stitch. Bring the needle up to the edge of the anchor stitch, double back through it, and then pass the needle through the fabrics to create your second stitch. Catch the loop of thread with your needle and pass it through, pulling the thread taut before the loop tightens, so it forms a second stitch.

3. Continue stitching forward, catching the loop of thread with the needle and creating more blanket stitches until you reach the end of the fabric.

4. When you turn a corner, simply continue to stitch the same way, letting the thread extend around the corner and then adding a new stitch to continue.

If you run out of thread, bury the knot between the two layers of fabric and begin with another anchor stitch.

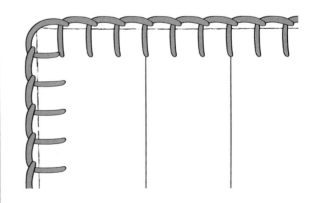

Backing Quilts

To finish the quilts in this book, you'll add a simple backing and stitch around the perimeter, rather than binding them like a traditional cotton patchwork quilt. Unlike traditional cotton quilts, no batting is used for the quilts in this book.

When choosing a backing fabric, make sure the fabric is not too heavy for your finished quilt. For example, I paired a lightweight plaid quilt top with a medium-weight **Square-Within-a-Square Plaid Quilt** on p. 80. For the **Improvisational Patchwork Quilt** on p. 84, I paired a heavier patchwork top with a very lightweight backing.

Here's how I back my quilts:

Attaching the Backing

1. Place your backing fabric right side up on a floor or large, flat surface, and make sure it's smooth and lying flat. Place your pieced quilt top over it, right side down, with edges aligned with the backing fabric. The backing fabric can be larger than the top; you can trim it after sewing.

2. Pin the two layers together around the perimeter, leaving an opening for turning as specified in the project instructions, and stitch all around the perimeter, backstitching at the beginning and end of the seam and leaving the opening unsewn.

3. Clip the corners and trim any excess backing fabric. Carefully turn the quilt right side out, shaking it gently, and guiding the corners open to neat points.

tip

When you turn a project like a quilt or a bag right side out, bulky seams can show or change the line of that section. Clip corners or curves to reduce that bulk for a smoother finished project.

4. Press and pin the perimeter of the quilt, turning the raw edges under to match the quilt edges. The quilt is now right side out; raw edges are now at the opening. Press and pin.

Perimeter Stitching

This final "victory lap" of stitching creates a simple, neat edge for a pieced wool quilt.

1. Using a standard or longer stitch length, stitch around the entire perimeter of your pinned quilt, removing pins as you near them and turning 90-degree angles at each corner. Stitch very close to the edge, catching both layers of the quilt evenly and catching the raw edges inside the quilt.

2. When you reach the end of the perimeter stitching, backstitch a few stitches to hold the seam and trim threads. Shake your quilt out gently. Now it's ready to use!

Installing Invisible Zippers

I learned this fantastic basic technique from quilter Katie Pedersen. I adapted her technique for sewing with wool.

1. Measure and mark the center of your zipper with ink or fabric marker on the back of the zipper. Measure and cut a small notch in the bottom center of your two pillow panels. You'll use these to neatly match your zipper and pillow panels as you sew.

note If you accidentally leave your zipper closed when sewing around the pillow cover, you'll need to carefully open the side seam with a seam ripper and unzip the zipper, then re-sew.

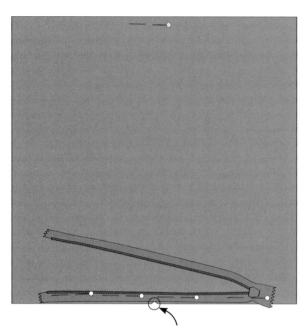

2. Open your zipper and place the lower half of it, teeth down, along the bottom of the right side of the front pillow panel. Match the notch with the mark on the back of your zipper. Pin in place.

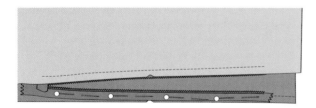

3. Using an invisible zipper foot, stitch the zipper, working from the open end to the zipper pull. Backstitch to hold the seam.

4. Now match, pin, and stitch the other half of your zipper the same way to the right side of the back pillow panel.

5. Leave your zipper at least two-thirds unzipped. Place the two panels together, right sides facing. Pin around the three open sides of the pillow, extending the zipper ends out of the pinned section so they will be tucked inside the finished pillow cover.

6. Stitch from one end of the zipper all the way around the perimeter to the other, backstitching at the beginning and end to hold the seam, and turning corners with right angles.

7. Clip corners and gently turn your pillow cover right side out again. Tuck a pillow form inside and zip it up.

Centering Designs

Carefully spotlighting and centering beautiful Pendleton jacquard designs makes a finished sewing project beautiful. There are two ways to center your designs:

Pattern Pieces

Trace pattern pieces onto semi-opaque dotted paper. Mark pattern pieces with a center line for planning your cutting so that you will know where to place the pattern on the fabric when cutting.

tip

Using scraps or off-center cuts can also be a wonderful design element, as in the **Improvisational Patchwork Quilt** on p. 84. The beauty of the patterns is almost more evident when they're seen in parts instead of a perfect, symmetrical whole.

Marking Fabric

Measuring and marking the fabric itself both horizontally and vertically with chalk or pins help keep the heart of the design nicely centered. Remember that you'll lose a small border to the seam allowance—often ½ in. on each side—so keep that in mind when centering and cutting your fabric.

Working with Plaids

Here are a few tips from Amy Alan, designer of the **Modern Plant Hanger** on p. 42, for working with plaid designs.

- Carefully look over the stripes on your plaid. Folding the fabric lengthwise, crosswise, and diagonally will help you match up your stripes to see if your plaid is balanced or unbalanced. Be sure to check the colors of the fabric carefully, as uneven color is a sign of an unbalanced plaid.

- Generally, the dominant plaid line in your fabric is used down the center of your project. Drape your fabric over a chair and view it from across the room to find the dominant line or color in the plaid. If the colors appear to be evenly distributed, then any of the stripes could be used as the main focal point in your project.

- Before purchasing your fabric, consider how large the plaid repeat is. If the fabric has a large repeat, you will need to buy extra yardage to correctly match up the plaid stripes.

- Check your fabric to make sure that both sides can be used, as one side may have a nap or texture to it, which will require more planning before cutting.

Working with Leather

Meredith Neal is an expert when it comes to working with leather. Use these tips when making Meredith's **Modern Embroidered Tote** on p. 104, or for any other project you're working on that uses leather.

- Choose the right needles and presser foot. Leather needles have a cutting point at the tip: This triangle design allows for easy piercing through leather.

- Use a leather-friendly presser foot. The metal sole of your standard foot will stick, causing irregular stitching. There are several options for "leather feet." The most versatile is a Teflon® or coated foot, which will slide easily over the leather. You could also try a walking foot, which would "walk" across the leather, or a roller foot, which would "roll" across the leather.

- Increase your stitch length to about 4 stitches per inch.

- Since you are unable to pin leather without leaving holes, consider using washable tape or clips, such as Clover Wonder Clips, to hold leather together.

Binding

See the **Classic Blanket** on p. 70 for a guide to sewing wool binding.

Felting

You can lightly felt many wools (including most Pendleton wools) for sewing or crafting in a home washing machine. Just wash your wool yardage or smaller pieces as part of a regular load of laundry with gentle soap and warm water once or twice, then dry on a medium setting for a cozy, soft effect. The wool will shrink, so be forewarned, but this method is perfect for a project like the **Men's Scarf** on p. 118.

3 Modern Home Basics

William Morris once said, ***"Have nothing in your house you do not know to be useful, or believe to be beautiful."*** My favorite sewing projects are both practical and lovely to look at—a pretty little set of nesting boxes, a vividly striped rug, modern plant hangers, or a graphic botanical table runner you'll use all year round.

Leaf Table Runner

DIFFICULTY
TECHNIQUES Reverse appliqué, Topstitching (p. 18), Hand stitching (p. 11), Running stitch (p. 18)

Reverse appliqué is a fun technique to play with. Stack two or more wools together, and then cut shapes from the top layers to reveal the layers underneath. Here, beautiful leaf cutouts make a nice framework for simple hand stitching. You can easily size this project up or down to fit your table. Cut any rectangle size that fits, and feel free to shrink or expand the leaf pattern on a photocopier. Designed by Diane Gilleland.

FABRIC

- Pendleton Eco-Wise Wool
  (or upholstery-weight wool) in
  Geranium and Reef

YOU'LL NEED

- ½ yd. each of two coordinating
  Eco-Wise Wool fabrics
- Coordinating thread
- DMC #502 and #815 or other
  pearl cotton embroidery thread in
  coordinating colors
- Leaf pattern (p. 130)
- Card stock
- Water- or air-soluble fabric marker
- Crewel embroidery needle
- Scissors
- Quilting ruler
- Rotary cutter and cutting mat
- Pins
- Sewing machine
- Steam iron

tip

This project requires a little precise cutting, so your scissors should be very sharp. You may find, too, that smaller scissors are easier to maneuver around the leaf shapes than large ones.

Make the Table Runner

1. Using a ruler and rotary cutter, cut a 13-in. by 47-in. rectangle from each piece of wool.

2. Copy the leaf pattern (p. 130) onto card stock several times and carefully cut the leaves out. These will be your tracing patterns, and it's easiest to work with at least three of them, so you can clearly see the placement of the leaves on the runner.

3. Lay the wool you'll be using for the top layer of the runner flat on your worksurface. Starting at one end, place the leaf patterns over the wool, arranging them as you like. Carefully trace the outline of each leaf onto the wool. Remove the patterns, move them along the runner to a new spot, and trace them again. Repeat this process until you've covered the surface of the runner with leaf tracings. You can see Diane's leaf arrangements on p. 29.

4. Carefully cut away each leaf shape. Start by pinching a fold in the center of the leaf and making a small clip inside the shape. Then cut to your traced line, and then along that traced line. Be careful not to cut past these lines at the corners. Repeat this process to cut away the remaining leaves.

5. Pin the two pieces of wool together, lining up all four edges. The bottom layer will show through the cutouts you made in the top layer. Use plenty of pins all over the runner to keep the layers from shifting.

tip

Skim your needle through the top layer of wool instead of trying to pass it through both layers. This will make it much easier—and faster—to embroider the edges.

6. Machine-stitch through both layers, 1/8 in. from the edge of each leaf cutout. Remove the pins and press the runner to smooth it out to the edges. Re-pin the layers together, using fewer pins than you did in step 5.

7. Machine-stitch 1/8 in. from the four outer edges of the runner.

8. Trace vein lines in each leaf with a water- or air-soluble fabric marker, making them a little different on each leaf. Stitch over the vein lines with pearl cotton using a running stitch.

9. Use a ruler and water- or air-soluble fabric marker to draw a border 3/4 in. from the outer edges of the runner. Embroider over this line with a running stitch.

10. Embroider around each leaf with a running stitch about 1/4 in. from the cut edges, again skimming through the top layer of wool only. Remove all marks, then press the finished runner.

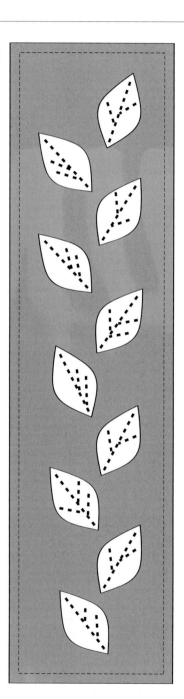

Patchwork Draft Snake

TECHNIQUES Patchwork (p. 14), Topstitching (p. 18), Hand stitching (p. 11)

This quick little draft snake is as cute as it is practical, and it's the perfect way to use wool scraps left over from bigger projects. Lining a chilly doorway keeps cold air out and makes your house warm and cozy, and you can stitch one up in less than an hour!

FABRICS
- Pendleton Merino Fabric (or soft, midweight wool)
- Pendleton Jacquard Blanket Fabric (or blanket-weight wool)

YOU'LL NEED
- Assorted solid or jacquard blanket-weight wool fabric scraps, at least 7 in. wide (I used solid colors in orange and blue)
- Measuring tape
- Sewing machine
- Steam iron
- Pins
- Needle and thread
- Natural cat litter (I used one made from corn)

Make the Draft Snake

1. Measure your doorway. Add 2 in. to yield the length of your simple draft snake pattern, and write your final measurement here: _____.

2. Choose a mix of wool scraps of varying lengths, and trim each of them to 7 in. wide. Arrange them in a color pattern you like, and then join them with a ½-in. seam allowance so your patchwork section measures 7 in. wide by _____ in. long. (Fill in the blank with your number from step 1.)

7 in.

Width of door + 2 in.

3. Press each seam to one side with a steam iron (p. 13) and topstitch (p. 18) each seam to catch all layers and hold them flat.

4. Fold the patchwork section in half lengthwise with wrong sides facing. Press and pin it together at one short end and all along the long side, leaving the other short end open. Stitch all along the pinned edges with a ½-in. seam allowance, backstitching at the beginning and end to hold the seam.

tip

You can fill your draft snake with dried rice or beans, but they may mold if the snake gets damp or wet. I used a natural-ingredient cat litter made of coarsely ground dried corn.

5. Turn the snake right side out and fill it close to the top with natural cat litter. Fold the raw edges of the opening down by ½ in. and pin them together. Hand-stitch the opening closed with invisible or matching thread.

3 in.

Width of door + 1 in.

6. Place the draft snake in front of your door to block cold air and drafts from rushing into your house!

Caring for Your Draft Snake

Wool repels dust and dirt nicely, so if you keep your draft snake brushed or swept, it should stay clean and vibrant. You may want to use white and cream colors sparingly for practicality, but as you can see, I included light blue in my patchwork sequence that has held up beautifully for two years and counting.

Nesting Boxes

DIFFICULTY 🐑 🐑
TECHNIQUE Blanket stitch (p. 19)

This set of three nesting boxes is one of my favorite projects to sew. The boxes are graduated sizes (4 in., 5 in., and 6 in. across), so they fit inside one another for easy stacking. Mix plaids, solids, or any other combination of fabrics for the outside and lining of each box, or use the same fabric for an understated and lovely effect. Blanket-stitching the boxes goes quickly, but has the meditative appeal of knitting or crochet. The process can be as enjoyable as the result!

FABRICS

- Pendleton Eco-Wise Wool (or upholstery-weight wool) in Doe, Bamboo, and Reef
- Assorted Pendleton Plaids (or men's shirting wool)

note I don't recommend a broader-weave jacquard fabric for this project because the edges get a little shredded when you blanket-stitch. Eco-Wise Wool flannel, plaids, and other lightweight flannels are all perfect choices, as are other closely woven fabrics.

YOU'LL NEED

- Small quantities of fabrics for the outside and lining of each box (see cutting instructions for exact amounts)
- Heavy double-sided interfacing, such as 72F Peltex® II
- DMC #642 or other pearl cotton
- Scissors or rotary cutter
- Quilting ruler
- Cutting mat
- Steam iron
- Sewing machine with neutral thread color

FABRIC CUTTING CHART

| | Interfacing | | Outer and Lining | |
	PIECES	MEASUREMENTS	PIECES	MEASUREMENTS
Small (4 in.)	1	4 in. × 4 in.	1	8 in. × 4 in.
	4	2 in. × 4 in.	2	2 in. × 4 in.
Medium (5 in.)	1	5 in. × 5 in.	1	10 in. × 5 in.
	4	2½ in. × 5 in.	2	2½ in. × 5 in.
Large (6 in.)	1	6 in. × 6 in.	1	12 in. × 6 in.
	4	3 in. × 6 in.	2	3 in. × 6 in.

Make the Nesting Boxes

note These instructions and diagrams are for the large box, but each one is made the same way, so use the same techniques for each size.

Cut and prepare your fabrics and interfacing:

Press each of your 12-in. by 6-in. and 3-in. by 6-in. fabrics.

1. Prepare your box components by placing your 12-in. by 6-in. piece of outer fabric right side down on your ironing board. Carefully place your 6-in. by 6-in. square of interfacing in the center (which will be the box base), then add two of your 3-in. by 6-in. pieces at each end. These pieces will be two of the sides.

2. Place your 12-in. by 6-in. piece of lining fabric over the outer fabric and interfacing so they align neatly. Using a steam iron, press the stack of fabrics and interfacing until they are fused. Carefully flip the stack over so the outer fabric is at the top and press again.

3. Arrange and press the remaining 3-in. by 6-in. pieces of outer fabric, interfacing, and lining in the same way to create the remaining two sides.

4. Using a neutral or matching thread color, edgestitch around each box section. For each of the single sides, simply stitch a rectangle outline. For the joined box base and sides section, stitch a rectangle outline and then carefully stitch along the edges where the sides meet the base. Trim any errant edges with a quilting ruler and rotary cutter or scissors to straighten.

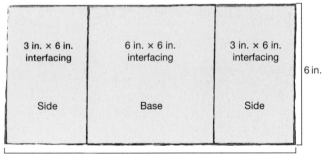

5. Bend the joined section at the stitch lines, lining the sides up, to form a simple box shape. Arrange one side rectangle to meet the open side space, aligning them like a puzzle.

6. Begin blanket-stitching to join the first side rectangle to the body of the box, starting with a sturdy double stitch at one top corner and continuing down the edge of the box (A). When you reach the base (B), adjust your box alignment if needed and continue stitching across, turning the second corner (C) the same way to stitch up to the opposite top edge of the side. Finish with two sturdy stitches and bury your knot (D). Repeat this process to join the second side rectangle to the opposite side of the box. Instead of knotting at the top edge, continue blanket-stitching around the perimeter of the box, finishing with two sturdy stitches and burying the knot.

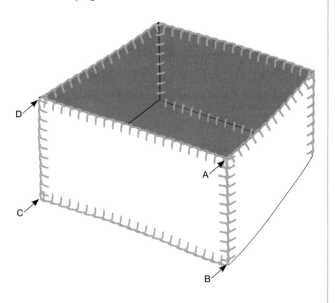

7. Press each side of the box with a hot steam iron to straighten. The sides you attach may have a slight curve, and the ones that were joined to the base from the beginning may have an opposite curve, but they will straighten nicely when pressed.

8. Repeat these instructions to make small and medium boxes—or any sizes of your choice. These boxes are exactly half as tall as they are wide, but you can adjust sizes and ratios if you'd like.

Party Pennants

DIFFICULTY 🐑

TECHNIQUES Tearing and cutting wool (p. 13), Wool binding (p. 71, step 3)

This cheerful set of triangular pennants is one of the simplest, quickest projects to sew, but it's perfect for a party, decorating a child's room, or any special event. I used four solid colors of blanket-weight wool—orange, light blue, medium blue, and oatmeal— and randomized my color placement for a casual effect, but you could use any wool fabrics that appeal to you, whether it's alternating two colors for a more organized approach, using a much bigger array of patterns or hues, or anything in between.

FABRIC
- Pendleton Blanket Fabric (or blanket-weight wool)

YOU'LL NEED
- Wool fabric in colors of your choice; I used orange, oatmeal, and two shades of blue
- Wool felt binding tape (about 3 in. per pennant, plus 6 in. extra for tails on each end)
- Party Pennants pattern (p. 131)
- Scissors or rotary cutter
- Cutting mat
- Pattern paper
- Pins
- Thread to match binding
- Quilting ruler
- Sewing machine
- Steam iron

note I cut 60 pennants to make a strand that was 10 yd. long, but this project is completely flexible. Twelve pennants make a strand about 2 yd. long, 30 pennants make a strand about 5 yd. long, and so on.

Make the Pennant

1. Trace and cut out the Party Pennants pattern on p. 131. You can cut out as many triangles as you want for your strand of pennants.

2. To cut individual pennant colors, simply pin your pattern to wool fabric. Cutting on grain is easiest, but you can cut on the bias if you'd like to capture that effect. Cut the triangle shape out.

   To cut a larger number of pennants in each color, cut or tear a 3-in.-wide strip of the fabric and then place your pennant pattern at one end. Use a rotary cutter to cut the first triangle, then flip your pattern to match the new diagonal edge. Continue cutting until you have the desired number of pennants.

3. Press each triangle until neat and flat.

4. Press your wool felt binding tape lengthwise using steam so there is a sharp, neat crease at the center point. Leaving a binding tail of a few inches, begin tucking and pinning your triangles into the fold of the binding. Use whatever color arrangement appeals to you, whether it's exact repetition or randomizing. I mixed mine up without repeating; my only rule was not to place the same color side-by-side.

5. When you're pleased with the arrangement, stitch the binding from end to end, starting with the edge of one tail. I used a large zigzag stitch. Trim the threads and you're ready to hang!

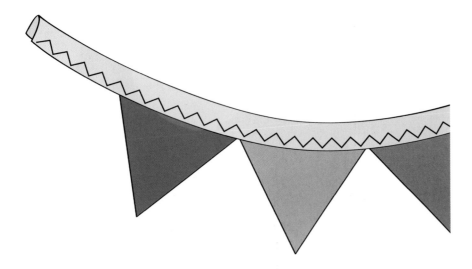

Square Coasters and Trivet

DIFFICULTY 🐑

TECHNIQUES Log cabin piecing (p. 14), Topstitching (p. 18), Hand stitching (p. 11), Blanket stitching (p. 19)

This simple set of a square-within-a-square trivet and coaster box with four reversible coasters is easy to make with two colors of Eco-Wise Wool. Like the Leaf Table Runner project (p. 26), I used Geranium and Reef for a nice contrast, then mixed hand and machine stitching for a simple, pretty effect.

FABRICS
- Pendleton Eco-Wise Wool (or upholstery-weight wool) in Geranium and Reef

YOU'LL NEED
- ⅓ yd. each of two Eco-Wise Wool fabrics
- Double-sided fabric bonding sheets, such as Phoomph in the stiff weight or other heavy interfacing
- 9-in. square of heat-resistant liner, such as Insul-Bright®
- Fabric pen
- Scissors
- Rotary cutter
- Quilting ruler
- Cutting mat
- Pins
- Sewing machine with coordinating threads
- Steam iron
- DMC #815 or other pearl cotton
- Crewel needle

Make the Trivet

1. Cut a 4-in. center square in red and a 3-in. by 24-in. strip of aqua wool. Using the basic log cabin piecing technique (p. 14), add the aqua logs around the red center square, working clockwise and using a ½-in. seam allowance. Press.

2. Topstitch around the inner edge of the aqua square.

3. Cut a 2-in. by 36-in. strip of red wool and add a second layer of logs the same way as the first. Press and topstitch around the edge of the red square.

4. Align the square of heat-resistant liner to the center back of the now-10-in. block and pin in place. Hand-quilt the block with a running stitch along the inner and outer edge of the aqua logs square, knotting securely at the back.

5. Cut a 10-in. square of the red wool and a 9-in. square of double-sided fabric bonding sheet. Peel away one side of the paper and place the bonding sheet on the center of the larger square, adhering it to the wrong side of the fabric. (If you are using interfacing instead, press with an iron to fuse it.)

6. Peel away the second side of the paper and press the back of the quilt block against the top of the adhesive bonding sheet square so the heat-resistant liner section meets it.

7. Blanket-stitch around the edge of the trivet using a coordinating pearl cotton.

Make the Coaster Box

1. Cut a 4-in. square of red wool and a 2½-in. by 20-in. strip of aqua wool. Use the basic log cabin piecing method to add the aqua logs around the red center square, working clockwise and using a ½-in. seam allowance, to yield a 7-in. quilt block. Press.

2. Topstitch just around the aqua square with coordinating thread. Hand-stitch a running stitch using red pearl cotton, just as you did on the trivet.

3. Cut a 7-in. square of red wool and a 7-in. square of Phoomph for the back of the box. Peel away one side of the paper to adhere the Phoomph to the wrong side of the red wool square. Peel away the other side and align the quilt block over the Phoomph, pressing them together. If using interfacing, fuse with an iron.

4. Use a fabric pen and quilting ruler to mark 1¼-in. squares at each corner of the block. Neatly cut corners away using a rotary cutter and quilting ruler.

5. Beginning with two sturdy stitches at one inner corner as marked, hold and blanket-stitch the first two sides together at one corner, working from the bottom to the top to join them. Stitch across the top edge to the next open corner, align the two edges of the second cutout, and stitch down to the bottom of the box. Knot securely and bury the knot.

6. Continue blanket-stitching the same way, joining the sides at the cutouts and stitching along the perimeter of the box, until all edges are blanket-stitched.

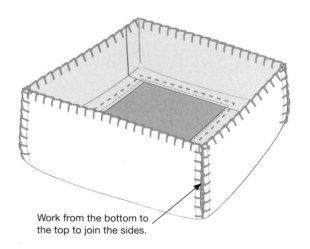

Work from the bottom to the top to join the sides.

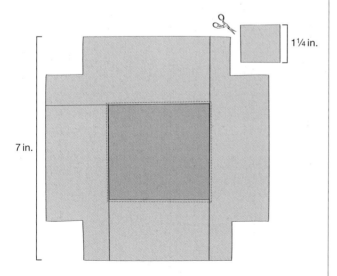

7 in.

1¼ in.

Make the Coasters

1. Cut four 4-in. squares each in red wool, aqua wool, and Phoomph.

2. Align one piece of red wool to the top of each square of Phoomph. Flip them over and align one square of aqua wool to the other side.

3. Blanket-stitch the perimeter of each coaster in red pearl cotton, knotting securely at the end and burying the knot.

Pendleton's Classic Advertisements

By 1956, Pendleton's ever-popular '49er was offered in no fewer than 20 different plaids, and the expanded women's wear line (now grown to include skirts, dresses, suits, and coats) was regularly advertised in *Vogue, McCall's, Glamour, The Saturday Evening Post, Seventeen*, and *Women's Wear Daily*. Longtime Pendleton illustrator Ted Rand created a series of perfectly of-the-moment advertisements for both the men's and women's wear lines from his studio on Whidbey Island in Washington. His illustrations were instantly recognizable for their graceful lines and striking use of color. Many referenced the beauty of the rugged Pacific Northwest and its endless inspirations for this western company, while always reinforcing the quality of the clothing and its timeless appeal.

Provided courtesy of Pendleton Woolen Mills

Modern Plant Hanger

DIFFICULTY 🐑 🐑
TECHNIQUES Cutting (p. 13), Topstitching (p. 18), Working with plaids (p. 22)

This stylish, modern wool plant hanger is equally striking in solids, plaids, or jacquard fabrics. If you do use a patterned wool, you can spotlight a stripe or another section of the design, as Amy did. Hanging a grouping of two or three of these in different fabrics looks especially beautiful! Designed by Amy Alan.

FABRICS

- Pendleton Blanket Fabric (or blanket-weight wool); Amy used two different plaids

YOU'LL NEED

- ¼ yd. of blanket fabric
- Modern Plant Hanger pattern (p. 132)
- Scissors
- Chalk
- Thread
- Large ¼-in. eyelets
- ⅜-in. by 44-in. strips of leather OR 2½ yd. of ½-in.-wide twill tape
- Planter with 6-in.-wide mouth, 5 in. tall (IKEA® Kardemumma planters are perfect)
- 90/14 gauge sewing machine needle
- Sewing machine
- Pins
- Steam iron
- Wooden clapper (optional)
- Seam roll (optional)

Make the Plant Hanger

1. Trace and cut out the three Modern Plant Hanger pattern pieces on pp. 132–133. Cut out four of the plant hanger side pieces, one bottom circle, and one planter base guide in blanket fabric, spotlighting any design you'd like to center. Mark the eyelet position on the outside of the side section, the notches on the bottom circle, and the outline of the tab location with chalk. If your fabric has a plaid stripe, be sure to check that you are matching plaids correctly around the body of the hanger.

2. Sew three of the plant hanger sides together, using a ¼-in. seam allowance and a medium stitch length. A walking foot (also called an even-feed foot) may help you to guide the pieces through your sewing machine. Press the seams open, using the wool setting on your iron, with plenty of steam. A wooden clapper can help to press the seams down.

3. Topstitch the seam allowance on either side of the seam, stitching ⅛ in. away from the side panel seam.

4. Insert the four eyelets at each eyelet marking on the top of the side pieces, following the eyelet package instructions.

5. Sew, press, and topstitch the last side piece's seam. A seam roll will be helpful for pressing open the seam allowances. It will be easiest to topstitch this seam from the top down, being careful not to stretch out the top or bottom of the side pieces.

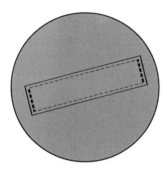

6. Topstitch the long sides of the tab piece to help keep it from stretching. Stitch the tab to the middle of the bottom circle by sewing the short ends down. Be sure to remember to backstitch to secure your stitching.

7. With right sides together, pin the bottom circle to the side pieces, matching each notch with a seamline. Sew this seam with a ¼-in. seam allowance.

8. Fold the top ½-in. edge of the side pieces toward the inside of the planter and press. Stitch ¼ in. away from the pressed edge, being careful not to bring the needle down on the edge of an eyelet.

9. Feed the leather or twill tape through one eyelet, through the bottom tab, and up the side of the planter through the opposing eyelet. Knot the strips together above the planter and hang.

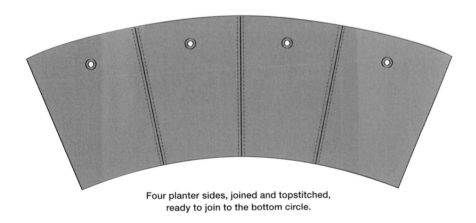

Four planter sides, joined and topstitched, ready to join to the bottom circle.

Wool Binding Kitchen Rug

DIFFICULTY 🐑 🐑
TECHNIQUES Tearing and cutting wool (p. 13), Topstitching (p. 18), Blanket stitch (p. 19)

Add a cozy burst of color to that well-traveled spot in front of your kitchen sink—or anywhere else you choose—with this fun wool binding rug. This rug was designed in a beautiful palette of red, steel blue, and gray, but you can adapt this pattern arrangement to reflect your favorite colors. Designed by Haley Pierson-Cox.

FABRICS
- Pendleton Melton (or jacket-weight wool); Haley used gray
- Pendleton Wool Binding (or wool felt binding); Haley used red, steel blue, and gray

YOU'LL NEED
- 4½ yd. red wool binding
- 5½ yd. steel blue wool binding
- 6½ yd. gray wool binding
- 30-in. by 18-in. rectangle of melton wool in a coordinating color
- Measuring tape
- Quilting ruler
- Scissors
- Pins
- Sewing machine
- Steam iron
- Thread in a dark neutral color
- Gray worsted-weight yarn
- Sharp darning needle
- Sewing needle

Assemble the Rug Top

1. Cut the wool binding into the following pieces, each 18 in. long:
   Red: 8 strips
   Steel blue: 10 strips
   Gray: 12 strips

2. Select a red strip and a steel blue strip—the first two stripes in the rug—and place the steel blue (#2) strip directly on top of the red strip (#1), ensuring that the ends and side edges line up perfectly. Pin in place. Use the full diagram on p. 48 for reference.

3. Using a ¼-in. seam allowance, sew the two strips together along the right edge with your sewing machine. Once the two strips are sewn together, lay the strips flat and use a steam iron to press the seam open.

4. Flip over the first two pieces of the rug top so that the seam is on the back, then pin a gray strip (#3) in place on top of the steel blue strip, lining up the right side edge of the gray strip to the unsewn edge of the steel blue strip. The top and bottom edges of the strips should now line up. If they don't, gently stretch the felt as needed to make the lengths equal.

5. Sew the blue strip (#2) and gray strip (#3) together along the right edge with a ¼-in. seam allowance. Unfold the strips so that all three lie flat, then press the second seam open on the back of the rug top.

note When the three stitched strips are laid flat, the seam that you sewed in step 3 and the seam that you sewed in step 5 should both be on the same side of the piece. This is the back side of the rug's top.

6. Following the guide below, continue sewing the remaining strips to the rug top with a ¼-in. seam allowance, pressing the seams open on the back with a steam iron after each new strip is added. The wool binding is 1½ in. wide so each individual stripe should measure 1 in. wide after both side edges are sewn.

7. When all 30 wool binding strips have been sewn together, carefully use the steam iron to press the finished rug top flat, then stretch it gently by hand to expand it to its full width.

8. Trim ¼ in. off the unsewn edges on the first and last strips. Wool can be difficult to press completely flat once it's sewn together, so if your rug top measures smaller than 30 in. by 18 in. at this point, skip this step and leave the extra length at the ends.

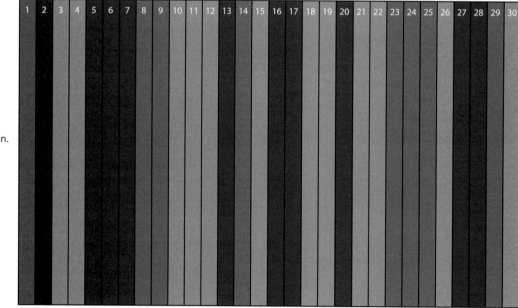

30 in.

18 in.

Join the Rug Top to the Rug Base

9. Place the rug top on top of the 30-in. by 18-in. rectangle of blanket-weight wool (the rug base) with the seam side facing down. Align all sides and pin in place, gently stretching as needed to ensure that all edges line up.

10. Starting at the center of the rug top and working your way toward both edges, use a needle and thread to baste the rug top and the rug base together along each rug top seam using large stitches.

11. Use a sewing machine to sew the top and base together along those seams. Remove the basting stitches.

Finish the Rug

12. Blanket-stitch around the outside edges with gray worsted-weight yarn.

Optional: To add a no-slip grip to the bottom of the finished rug, sponge a layer of dimensional fabric paint onto the back of the rug. (Tulip® Dimensional Fabric Paint in a matte finish works well.)

4 Pillows and Upholstery

Sewing new pillows instantly adds a bright pop of color or a fresh, stylish look to any room in your home. Whether you choose an ultra-simple plaid design, a graphic modern cross, two very different takes on the always-striking chevron, or build a beautiful stand-alone ottoman, these projects make a statement.

Plaid Pillows

DIFFICULTY 🐑

TECHNIQUES Working with plaids (p. 22), Installing invisible zippers (p. 20)

You can use any wool fabric for these ultra-simple pillow covers, but I love the crispness of plaids, whether you cut your fabric on grain or on the bias to create an eye-catching diagonal design. An invisible zipper closure keeps the construction very quick, and the project can be scaled up or down for any sized pillow!

FABRICS

- Pendleton Flannel
  (or men's shirting wool)
- Pendleton Worsted
  (or light apparel-weight wool)
- Pendleton Jacquard Blanket
  Fabric (or midweight wool)

YOU'LL NEED

- Pillow form
- Fabric of your choice cut to
  same dimensions as pillow
  form (see step 1)
- Invisible zipper 1 in. shorter than
  your pillow form
- Sewing machine with invisible
  zipper foot and presser or
  ¼-in. foot
- Coordinating thread
- Quilting ruler
- Rotary cutter and cutting mat
- Steam iron
- Scissors
- Pins
- Chopstick

Cutting Fabric on the Bias

Cutting on the bias can result in an interesting diagonal design, as I did for my 12-in. pillow cover. To cut on the bias, just use a quilting ruler and rotary cutter to cut a square the correct size at a 90-degree angle instead of on grain, or make a paper pattern the correct size and pin that to your fabric, cutting around it with scissors or a rotary cutter.

Make the Pillow

1. Measure your pillow form and cut your fabric into two squares that are the same dimensions as the pillow form. For example, if you are using a 12-in. pillow form, cut two 12-in.-square pieces of wool, matching plaids if necessary. Press the pieces.

2. Choose which fabric edge will be the bottom (zipper) edge of the finished pillow. Measure and mark the exact center on each square. Clip a small V at that spot.

3. Use the invisible zipper instructions (p. 20) to stitch your zipper to the bottom edge of each fabric piece. Unzip it at least halfway or more, and then pin the edges of the bottom section and the other three sides of the pillow cover fabrics together, right sides facing and with zipper tape ends extending out from the pinned seam.

4. Stitch the pillow cover together all the way around the perimeter with a ½-in. seam allowance, backstitching at the beginning and end to hold the seam. Clip the corners to reduce fabric bulk and turn the pillow cover right side out through the open zipper, pushing the four corners out with a chopstick.

5. Place your cover over the pillow form and zip it closed. Hand-stitch any small openings at the beginning or end of the zipper.

Improvisational Chevron Bolster

DIFFICULTY 🐑 🐑 🐑

TECHNIQUES Tearing and cutting wool (p. 13), Patchwork (p. 14), Topstitching (p. 18), Installing invisible zippers (p. 20)

This scrappy chevron pillow features improvisational piecing and a modern attitude. A little planning and a couple of guidelines are all you need to create a unique and graphic project of your own. Designed by Sandie Holtman.

FABRIC

- Pendleton Melton (or jacket-weight wool)
- Jacquard Blanket Fabric (or mid-weight wool)
- Shirtweight Flannel (or men's shirting wool)

YOU'LL NEED

- ½ yd. of fabric (A) for pillow front
- 14½-in. by 28½-in. piece of fabric in a complementary color for the back of the pillow.
- Assortment of lightweight or jacquard wool fabric strips 2 in. to 4 in. wide and 24 in. long
- Quilting ruler
- Rotary cutter and cutting mat
- Thread to match or coordinate with front and back fabrics
- Sewing machine with presser foot and invisible zipper foot
- Pins
- Marking pencil
- 1 invisible zipper, 20 in. long
- Steam iron
- Chopstick or other smooth, pointy tool
- 14-in. by 28-in. pillow form

note Remember, a Pendleton fat quarter actually measures 18 in. by 24 in. to 30 in., so it's larger than a quilting cotton fat quarter, which measures 18 in. by 24 in.

Cut the Fabrics

1. Cut fabric (A) in the following dimensions:
   Large: 18 in. by 20 in.
   Medium: 18 in. by 15 in.
   Small: 18 in. by 10 in.

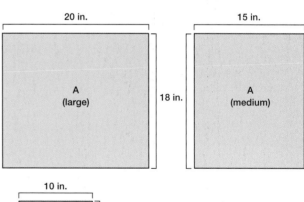

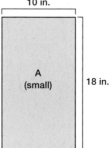

2. In order to create the chevron effect, directional strips are pieced. In this case, the largest background fabric is cut diagonally from top left to bottom right, and the other two are cut diagonally from bottom left to top right. Lay all the pieces out as indicated and mark the following:

Large piece: With 18-in. sides on the left and right, place a mark or pin 4 in. down from the top left. Mark 4 in. up from the bottom right.

Medium and small pieces: Lay out the piece, again with the 18-in. sides on the left and right. This time, pin or mark 4 in. up from the bottom left. Mark 4 in. down from the top right.

   Starting with the smallest piece, use a quilting ruler to match the two marks and rotary cut along the diagonal line. Repeat for other two pieces.

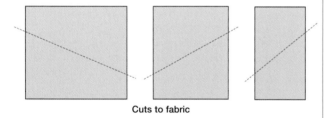

Cuts to fabric

Construct the Chevron

3. Separate the two pieces of the smallest section slightly. Lay a strip of contrasting fabric on the lower edge. Sew with a ½-in. seam allowance.

4. Press away from the contrasting fabric. Topstitch on the background fabric. Lay the top half of the background on the contrasting fabric strip, right sides together. Slide the fabric down about ½ in. on the diagonal. Pin and sew.

5. Press and topstitch. Trim the inset strip even with the sides of the background. Set aside. Stitch the two long strips together.

6. Repeat steps 3–5 for the medium piece, using two strips of fabric if desired. Sew those together lengthwise, then piece into the medium section. Set aside.

7. Repeat steps 3–5 for the large piece, keeping the 18 in. sides on the left and right, and the diagonal cut from top left to bottom right. Trim both sides of the large piece even.

8. From each side of the largest section, cut one strip 4 in. wide, leaving the center section uncut. Set aside the strips. Working with just the center section, measure up 1¼ in. from the contrast strip and cut another diagonal line.

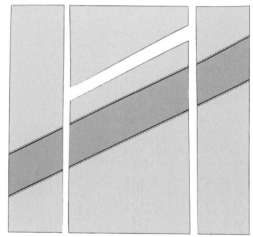

Fabric section with contrast insert

   Insert a second, narrower strip of fabric as before. Square one side, and cut two 4-in. strips.

   From the small piece, cut two 4-in. strips. From the medium piece, cut three 4-in. strips. You should now have four assorted strips with the diagonal running top left to bottom right and five assorted strips with the diagonal running bottom left to top right. Discard any extra fabric left over or use for another project.

9. Lay out the strips, alternating the direction of the diagonals to create an informal chevron. Keep the piecing centered horizontally on the pillow top.

Trimmed sections rearranged to form chevron design

10. Sew the strips together. Press seams open. Topstitch on either side of the seams.

Stitched sections of pillow front

11. Trim to 14½ in. by 28½ in.

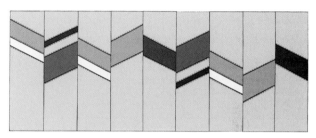

Trimmed pillow front

Install the Zipper

12. Follow the instructions on p. 20 for installing an invisible zipper. Begin by sewing the zipper to the pillow front, then join the zipper to the back panel of the pillow.

Finish the Pillow

13. Clip corners and trim any other uneven sections of the pillow panels. Turn pillow right side out, poke corners open with a chopstick or other smoothly pointed tool, and open the zipper all the way. Insert the pillow form. Zip it up and place it on your couch!

Appliqué Pillow

DIFFICULTY

TECHNIQUES Tearing and cutting wool (p. 13), Topstitching (p. 18)

This gorgeous appliqué pillow is just the thing for a stylish, modern living room. The chevron shape is perfectly suited to the graphic nature of the Pendleton fabric designs, and you can mix and match patterns and solids. This easy machine-appliqué technique is so versatile, and delivers so much style with minimal fabric yardage, that you'll want to use it on all of your appliqué projects! Designed by Anna Joyce.

FABRICS
- Pendleton Eco-Wise Wool (or upholstery-weight wool); Anna used charcoal gray
- Pendleton Jacquard (or mid-weight wool); Anna used yellow solid and Coyote Butte in black

YOU'LL NEED
- ¼ yd. fusible webbing
- ¾ yd. Eco-Wise Wool in charcoal gray for the pillow front
- ¾ yd. jacquard in yellow for pillow back and appliqué pieces
- Jacquard for contrast appliqué
- Chevron pattern (p. 134)
- 100% cotton thread to match appliqué fabrics
- 20-in.-square pillow form
- Scissors
- Pencil
- Pins
- Steam iron
- Sewing machine

note One side of the webbing is a very thin web of heat-sensitive glue; the other side is a paper that can be drawn on easily. It is transparent enough to see through and trace your pattern pieces with a pencil or pen.

Prepare the Fabrics

1. Cut one 20-in. square from the solid wool fabric of your choice for the front of the pillow.

   Cut two 20-in. by 16-in. rectangles of contrasting wool solid for the back of the pillow.

2. Trace seven chevron pattern pieces from the pattern on p. 134 onto the paper side of your fusible webbing and cut them out.

3. Cut out all the chevron shapes and use a hot steam iron to adhere them, glue side down, to the wrong side of your patterned and solid wool pieces.

4. Set your iron to the wool setting and make sure that there is plenty of steam.

tip

Do not peel the paper backing from the appliqué pieces until you are done fusing them onto your fabric and cutting them out. It is much easier to handle the appliqué pattern pieces when they still have the paper backing in place.

Apply the Appliqué Pieces

5. Following the guidelines on the pattern, place the chevron pieces onto your 20-in.-square piece of fabric. Once the chevrons are in place, use your iron to slowly set the pieces onto the pillow front. The heat from the iron will fuse your appliqué pieces to your pillow front, therefore eliminating the need for pins.

6. To prevent the edges of your appliqué pieces from fraying, sew around each individual appliqué piece with a tight zigzag stitch. Adjust your sewing machine until you have a zigzag with a short stitch length so that the stitching is nice and tight and will keep your wool from fraying.

7. Center the stitch over the outer edge of your appliqués and sew around the perimeter of each piece using a thread that is the same color as the appliqué fabric. The thread will hide flaws and make your finished pillow look cleaner and more professional.

8. When you have finished zigzag stitching around the perimeter of all of your appliqué pieces, give your finished pillow front a good pressing with the iron and set it aside.

Make the Pillow Back

9. On each of the 20-in. by 16-in. rectangles, fold over and press a ½-in. seam. Pin seam into place. Machine-stitch the center of the fold, creating a finished edge.

10. Place rectangles on top of your finished appliqué pillow front, right sides together, so that all sides are squared up and the seams of the envelope closure overlap.

11. Pin all sides together and sew around the edge of the pillow using a straight stitch and ½-in. seam allowance. Clip corners. Turn your pillow right side out and use your finger to poke out the corners.

12. You can now open the "envelope" that was formed at the back of your pillow by the overlapping rectangles. Place the pillow form inside.

Wool Cross Pillows

DIFFICULTY 🐑 🐑 🐑

TECHNIQUES Patchwork (p. 14), Topstitching (p. 18), Working with plaids; optional (p. 22), Centering designs; optional (p. 22), Installing invisible zippers (p. 20)

These simple pillows pair two soft contrasting wool fabrics for a graphic design that draws the eye. Topstitching and framing lend structure to the cross patchwork, and the gorgeous backing blanket pattern is a striking alternative—you'll flip this pillow over to show both sides for sure!

FABRICS

- Pendleton Plaid Flannel (or men's shirting wool); I used Umatilla Plaid
- Pendleton Eco-Wise Wool (or upholstery-weight wool); I used Bamboo
- Pendleton Blanket (or blanket-weight wool); I used Pecos Ivory

note Remember, a Pendleton fat quarter actually measures 18 in. by 24 in. to 30 in., so it's larger than a quilting cotton fat quarter. This is especially important in matching plaids for your cross.

YOU'LL NEED

- One fat quarter of fabric for the cross (A)
- One fat quarter of fabric for the background (B)
- One 17-in. square of blanket fabric for the back
- Scissors
- Measuring tape
- Quilting ruler
- Rotary cutter and cutting mat
- Thread to match or coordinate with fabrics (A) and (B)
- Sewing machine with presser foot and invisible zipper foot
- Pins
- Fabric marker
- One invisible zipper, 14 in. long
- Steam iron
- Chopstick or other smoothly pointed tool
- 16-in. pillow form

Cut the Fabrics

1. Cut fabrics to the following dimensions:

Fabric (A): One 6-in. by 14-in. strip and two 6-in. by 5-in. strips to form the cross.

note If you are using a plaid fabric for the cross, please see the note on p. 63 for a simple way to "match" plaids before cutting.

Fabric (B): Four 5-in. squares, two 2½-in. by 14-in. strips, and two 2½-in. by 17-in. strips. If using a fat quarter, I suggest cutting the long strips first, then the squares.

Fabric (C): Cut one 17-in. square. See "Centering Designs" (p. 22) for tips on intentionally spotlighting a graphic section of a blanket or jacquard design.

Press all pieces with a steam iron.

Construct the Pillow Front

2. Pin two 5-in.-square pieces of fabric (B) to the short side of each of your cross arms (6-in. by 5-in. pieces of fabric A), right sides facing. Stitch them together with a ½-in. seam allowance, backstitching at the beginning and end to hold the seam. Press the seams toward the cross arms center section.

3. Pin one cross-arm panel to one long side of your 6-in. by 14-in. cross body, right sides facing and matching plaids if necessary. Stitch them together. Repeat with the second cross-arm panel on the other side of the cross body. Press seams toward the center of the cross body.

4. Press the entire cross panel from the front and back, using a steam iron so the seams are neat and flat. Pin around the perimeter of the cross, catching the pressed seam underneath on the wrong side, and then topstitch all around the four 90-degree angles that define the cross's inner corners.

5. Pin one 2½-in. by 14-in. strip of fabric (B) to one cross-arm side of your pillow center, right sides facing, and stitch it on to "frame" the cross. Repeat with the other 14-in.-long strip on the other side. Press both seams toward the frames, away from the center.

6. Repeat step 5 to stitch the 2½-in. by 17-in. strips to the top and bottom of your pillow center, again pressing your seams away from the center cross section.

7. As you did in step 4, press your pillow panel, front and back. Pin around the square perimeter of the "frame," catching the pressed seam underneath. Topstitch all around it, turning corners to complete an entire square of topstitching.

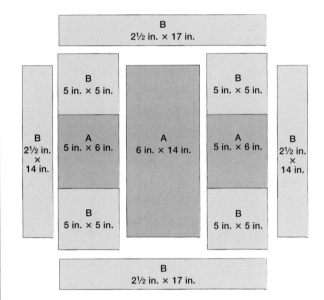

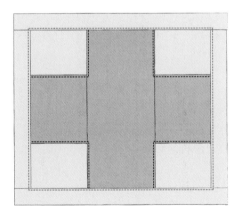

Install the Zipper

8. Follow the instructions on p. 20 for installing an invisible zipper.

9. Clip corners and trim any other wider or uneven sections of the pillow panels. Turn right side out and poke corners open with a chopstick or smoothly pointed tool. Open the zipper all the way and insert the pillow form.

Match Plaids In Fabric (A)

Cut a 6-in.-wide strip of plaid that is about 5 in. to 10 in. longer than 24 in. (the minimum needed for cutting the 14-in. and 5-in. sections that make up the cross).

Center the vertical cut on a dominant section of plaid to give a symmetrical feel to your design. You'll use this longer strip for both the cross body and arms so the plaid's "match" will not be precise, but it can be harmonious enough for the eye to read it smoothly.

Cut the two 6-in. by 5-in. pieces from one end first, and then arrange them at a right angle like the cross, aligning the 5-in. sides with the sides of the cross body.

Move the pieces up and down the remaining strip of fabric until you see a "match" of a dominant plaid. Pin the piece in place. Mark and use the midpoint of the cross arms as the center to trim the cross body to 14 in. long—7 in. above and below.

Cut Fabric for Two Coordinating Pillows

You may want to sew a coordinating set of pillows using each of the two fabrics as both cross and background in turn. For two pillows, you'll need approximately ½ yd. of fabrics (A), (B), and (C)

instead of fat quarters, but you will have nicely sized scraps left over for other projects. You'll cut both the cross and background sections from *each* fabric, instead of using only one for each.

Here's how to get the most out of your fabrics when making two coordinating pillows:

Cross body: Cut a 6-in. strip, centering any plaid or design vertically that you want to highlight, tearing the strip the width of the fabric. For each one, use the matching plaids technique described earlier to plan your cross if necessary.

Background: Cut a 5-in. strip, again tearing the strip the width of the fabric from both fabrics. Trim selvages.

Cut four 5-in. squares off one end with a rotary cutter. Set those aside.

Mark the midpoint of your remaining 5-in. strip at the 2½-in. mark, make a small cut, and tear it in half to create two long 2½-in.-wide strips. Cut a 14-in. and a 17-in. section from each one. You'll use these for your framing sections in steps 5 and 6.

Backing: Cut two 17-in. squares from your blanket fabric (C), centering any design you'd like to highlight.

Sew your pillows as described in the instructions.

Jacquard Cube Ottoman

DIFFICULTY 🐑 🐑 🐑
TECHNIQUES Simple woodworking

This cozy focus piece for your home is made with a graphic jacquard. The ottoman, on its wooden casters, is perfect for putting your feet up by the fire or can be a special seat for your favorite furry friend. This pattern requires the use of a drill and hammer, but it's about as simple as woodworking can get—especially if you ask your local hardware store to cut the lumber down to size for you. Designed by Amber Corcoran.

FABRICS

- Pendleton Jacquard (or mid-weight wool); Amber used Big Thunder Scarlet

YOU'LL NEED

- 1 yd. jacquard wool
- Coordinating thread
- Two packages (48 total) 7/16-in. or 1/2-in. decorative upholstery nails
- One 24-in. by 48-in. piece of 1/2-in. plywood cut into:
  – One 14-in. by 14-in. piece (A)
  – Four 13½-in. by 10-in. pieces (B) (see p. 65)
- One 24-in. by 24-in. piece of 1/2-in. plywood cut into:
  – One 17½-in. by 17½-in. piece (C) (see p. 65)
- 1½ yd. of 24-in.-wide, high-density 2-in. upholstery foam cut into:
  – Four 16-in. by 10½-in. pieces
  – One 18-in. by 18-in. piece (see p. 66)
- 12 Simpson Strong-Tie® #A21 angle brackets
- 64 #8 ½-in. Phillips-head sheet metal screws

- Four Liberty Non-Marring Wood
  Casters (100 mm) or other 5-in.
  legs or casters
- Drill
- ⅛-in. drill bit
- Phillips-head bit or screwdriver
- Tablesaw (if you did not purchase
  wood precut)
- Pencil
- Long serrated knife for cutting
  foam (if you did not purchase
  precut foam)
- 24-in. or longer acrylic ruler or
  straightedge
- Scissors
- Pins
- Sewing machine
- Steam iron
- Hammer

Precut Materials

If you don't have access to a tablesaw, you can
have your wood cut to size for you at a larger
hardware store. See right for a diagram of how
to cut your wood pieces. You can also order
your foam online, precut to the exact dimensions
needed.

1. Cut your wood pieces if you did not order your
   plywood precut.

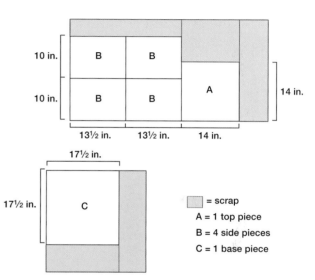

2. Bring together the shorter edges of two (B) pieces at
   a 90-degree angle, placing the cut end of one against
   the side of the other. Center an angle bracket on the
   outside of this corner. The longer side of the bracket
   will span the exposed end of one board so that the
   screws will fasten securely into the side of the other
   board. Mark the placement of the four holes. Drill pilot
   holes at your markings and attach the pieces with your
   angle bracket and four screws.

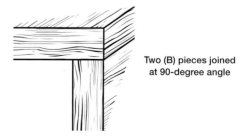

Two (B) pieces joined
at 90-degree angle

3. Repeat step 2 to join all four (B) boards together in a square.

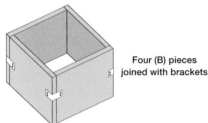

Four (B) pieces joined with brackets

4. Place piece (A) on top of the square you've made, lining up the corners and edges. Center a bracket on each side to secure the top. The longer side of the bracket will span the edge of piece (A), so that the screws will secure into the sides of the (B) pieces. Mark the holes and drill pilot holes as in step 2, then secure each bracket with four screws.

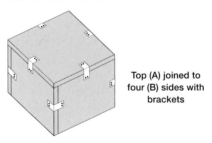

Top (A) joined to four (B) sides with brackets

5. Place your ottoman box on top of the base piece (C). Center it and make sure it is situated evenly from each side of the base. Center a bracket on each side to secure the top. The shorter sides of the brackets will be against the base piece (C). Mark the holes and drill pilot holes as in steps 2 and 4, then secure each bracket with four screws.

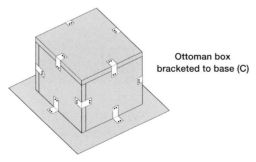

Ottoman box bracketed to base (C)

Cut the Foam and Fabric

6. If you don't have precut foam, use your straightedge to mark out your pieces. Work on a surface that won't be damaged by your knife. Line your straightedge up with your cut lines and use this as a guide for your long serrated knife. Use a gentle sawing motion—don't press down on the foam as you cut. Let the blade do the work; a gentle pressure will make a cleaner cut.

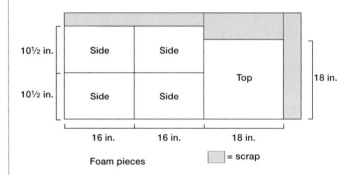

Foam pieces   = scrap

7. Cut fabric as follows:
   Top Piece (A): One 18½-in. by 18½-in. piece
   Side Piece (B): Four 18½-in. by 15-in. pieces
   Since each Pendleton Jacquard pattern is unique, you will want to decide how to cut your fabric based on the fabric pattern. Measure, mark, and make sure all your pieces fit before you begin cutting.

Make the Ottoman Cover

8. Pin one side piece (B) right sides together with the top piece (A). Start and end your seam ½ in. from the raw edge, and stitch the two pieces together, using a ½-in. seam allowance and backstitching at each end. Sew another (B) piece to opposite side of (A), starting and stopping ½ in. from the edge. Press seams away from the center, toward (B) pieces.

9. Place the third side piece (B) right sides together with (A) and, pushing the seam allowance of the previous (B) pieces out of the way, pin and stitch third (B) piece to (A), starting and stopping ½ in. from the edge as before. The other seam should be almost touching this seam.

10. Repeat for the fourth (B) piece. Press these seams toward (B).

11. Bring together two adjacent (B) side edges, right sides together. Push the seam allowance of piece (A) out of the way. Starting ½ in. from top edge and stopping 1½ in. from the bottom, sew the seam, backstitching at each end. Press these seams to one side.

   The three seams should meet on each corner, closing it up. If you still have a little hole here, use a needle and thread to hand-stitch this corner together before turning.

   Turn your cover right side out, and gently poke the corners out.

Assemble the Ottoman

12. Place foam onto the wooden ottoman structure.

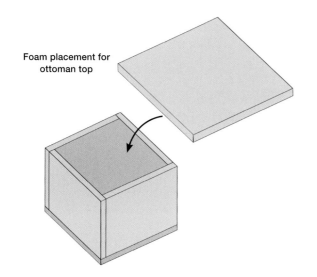

Foam placement for ottoman top

13. Hold foam in place as you slip the cover onto the foam box, making sure seams are lined up on the corners. Turn the box upside down. Clip a corner off the bottom of each side of the (B) pieces, only clipping in about ½ in. and down about 1½ in.

Clipped corner of each (B) piece

14. On the wooden base of the ottoman structure, mark the center of each side about ¾ in. in from the edge.

15. Starting on one side, fold the bottom of one (B) piece under 1 in. Pull it taut over the wooden base and tack at the center mark, making sure not to hit your bracket screws.

16. Tack the same (B) piece at each edge, about 1 in. from the corner of the wooden base. Place a tack between each side tack and the center tack. Once more, place a tack between each existing tack. You should have nine tacks in the first side, each about 2 in. apart.

17. Repeat for the opposite side. Repeat for sides 3 and 4, tucking the seam allowance under when you tack down the corners of these sides.

Attach the Casters

18. With your ottoman still upside down, place a caster at each corner as close to the corners as possible, but not on top of your fabric. Mark the screw holes. Drill pilot holes, trying not to go completely through the wood so as not to damage the foam. Attach each caster with four screws.

   Flip your finished ottoman over and have a seat!

5 Blankets and Beyond

If you've ever curled up with a Pendleton blanket, you know just how warm and comforting they are. Sew your own customized classic blanket, make a whole quilt in serene plaids, improvise a bold patchwork design from your favorite patterns, and bring a beautiful all-weather picnic blanket along on your next adventure.

Classic Blanket

DIFFICULTY 🐑 🐑

TECHNIQUES Wool binding (see step 3, below)

Make your own custom blanket in the pattern and size of your choice and edge it in lush wool felt binding for a gorgeously personalized gift. You can make a cozy lap blanket, a beautiful blanket for your bed, or anything in between.

FABRICS

- Pendleton Blanket Fabric (or blanket-weight wool); I used a large-scale plaid
- Pendleton Jacquard Blanket Fabric
- Pendleton Merino Fabric (or soft, mid-weight wool)
- Pendleton Wool Binding; I used navy

YOU'LL NEED

- Blanket-weight wool in the size of your choice, square or rectangular
- 1½-in. wool felt binding measuring the perimeter of your wool fabric plus 6 in.
- Steam iron
- Empty paper towel roll or sturdy cardboard
- Large zip-top bag
- Scissors
- Pins
- Sewing machine
- Coordinating thread
- Tag (optional)

Practice Makes Perfect

Practicing stitching your binding on a scrap is always a good idea. You can also try making a Soft Baby Blanket (p. 74) first for a more manageable practice piece. It's exactly the same technique, but working with a heavier and larger project like a full-size blanket is a bit more challenging.

Prepare the Fabrics

1. Trim your wool blanket fabric to a neat square or rectangle with perfectly straight edges and press it, particularly the edges, so there are no sizable wrinkles or creases.

2. Measure the perimeter of the blanket, add 6 in., and write the total here: _____. This will be the length of binding you'll need to edge your blanket. Cut the binding to this length.

3. Press the strip of wool felt binding in half lengthwise with a hot steam iron to create a sharp crease at exactly the center point, so the two edges are even and symmetrical. Continue pressing it to create flat, folded ¾-in.-wide binding, rolling the binding around a paper towel tube or a square, sturdy piece of cardboard to keep it organized and neat.

4. When you have reached the end of your binding, tuck the roll into a zip-top bag and pin the end of the binding to the roll to keep it from unrolling.

5. Prepare your blanket fabric: If the pattern is directional, choose its orientation. I like to start binding my blankets along a side edge. Pin your binding down starting 6 in. away from one corner, making sure the binding hugs the blanket snugly and evenly on both sides, all along the blanket edge to the opposite corner.

Attach the Binding

6. Arrange your blanket on your sewing table or a chair next to it, so that its weight doesn't pull it to the side as you sew. Using a longer stitch length (I use 4.5), stitch forward from the beginning of the binding to the far corner, close to the edge. Stitch slowly to catch both sides of the binding evenly. When you reach the far corner, stop sewing ¼ in. before the edge.

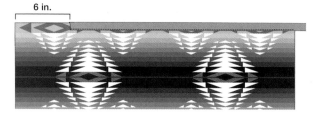

7. Press the first bound blanket edge with your iron. Fold the binding to make a neat triangular-fold corner, opening and then pressing this section carefully to preserve the crisp fold and making sure that the binding hugs the blanket neatly.

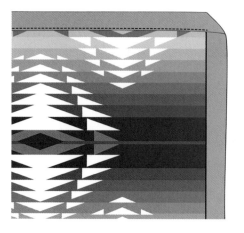

8. Pin the binding in place and hand-stitch the corner with large basting stitches in a contrasting thread color.

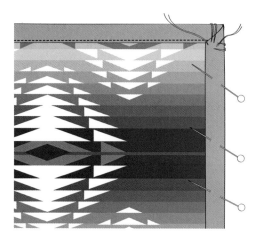

9. Continue pinning the neatly folded binding along the blanket's edge all the way to the next corner. Repeat steps 6, 7, and 8, always arranging your blanket so that its weight is secure, until you reach the fourth corner, close to where you began stitching originally.

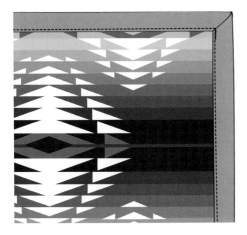

10. Create one last triangular-fold corner and hand-baste it as you did in step 8. Extend the binding past the original place you started sewing, so the two layers overlap at least 1 in. Trim the new binding at an angle.

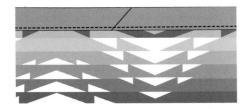

11. Pin the last section of binding down neatly, matching edges at the overlap. Stitch the last section down and backstitch to hold the seam. Press the entire binding section, working your way around the blanket, so it's neat and the fold is crisp.

12. Now it's time for my favorite part: the victory lap. Starting at the same section you chose in step 5, begin stitching the binding down again, but this time stitch very near the folded outside edge, instead of the inside edge. You can stitch around each corner, turning the blanket at right angles and shifting its weight as you go, without having to stop to pin or adjust the blanket binding. When you reach the original starting point again, backstitch for security. Trim all threads.

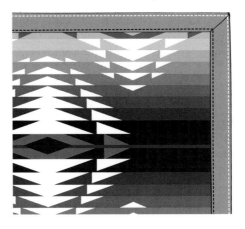

Optional: If you'd like to sew on a personal tag, pin it down near one corner—traditionally, it's the bottom right corner—and stitch it along all four sides.

Soft Baby Blanket

DIFFICULTY 🐑 🐑
TECHNIQUES Wool binding (p. 71, step 3)

This sweet two-sided baby blanket is the perfect gift for a new family. It's cozy, beautiful, and will last a baby well into toddlerhood and beyond. Choose ultra-soft merino for one side and a sturdier blanket fabric for the other—and make sure the fabrics are both washable, a necessity for little ones!

FABRICS
- Pendleton Merino Fabric (or soft, mid-weight wool); I used a large-scale plaid
- Pendleton Blanket Fabric (or soft, mid-weight wool); I used light blue
- Pendleton Wool Binding; I used white

YOU'LL NEED
- 36-in.-square piece of washable soft plaid merino wool (can be cut from one yard)
- 36-in.-square piece of washable blanket fabric (can be cut from one yard)
- 4½ yd. of wool felt binding
- Scissors
- Sewing machine
- Coordinating thread
- Pins
- Steam iron

Make the Blanket

1. Cut or tear a 36-in. square of each of your fabrics and press them. Align them exactly with wrong sides together, pinning if you like. Edgestitch around the perimeter.

2. Prepare your binding as you did for the Classic Blanket (p. 70). Follow the same general directions to bind the smaller two-layer baby blanket.

3. Give the blanket to your favorite new family with a card for their baby book.

If you have sizable scraps of either fabric left from a wider 1-yd. cut, you could make a matching plaid pillow (p. 52), or maybe a little cuddle toy or animal for the baby's first birthday.

Picnic Blanket

DIFFICULTY

TECHNIQUES Topstitching (p. 18)

This classic project is perfect for picnics all year round, whether you're going for a walk in the park or hiking in the mountains. Choose your favorite blanket fabric, back it with water-resistant, durable nylon, and make a simple, ingenious webbing handle with buckles to carry it along. Stacy and I both love the striking San Miguel fabric design, and I was so excited when she used it to make an absolutely beautiful, utterly modern version of the iconic picnic blanket. Designed by Stacy Brisbee.

FABRICS

- Pendleton Blanket Fabric (or blanket-weight wool); Stacy used San Miguel
- Water-resistant nylon

YOU'LL NEED

- 50-in. by 60-in. piece of blanket fabric (a 1½-yd. cut can be trimmed by 4 in. to make this size)
- 2 yd. water-resistant nylon
- 2 sets of 1-in. metal release buckles
- 2 yd. of 1-in. nylon webbing
- Pins
- Sewing machine
- Thread to match nylon
- Scissors
- Wooden matches

Bind the Blanket

1. Place the nylon fabric on a flat surface, coated side up. Place the blanket fabric over it, centering it so that the extra nylon fabric is even on all sides.

2. Create simple mitered corners with the nylon fabric by folding each corner of the nylon fabric toward the blanket fabric corner (see below).

Pin in place.

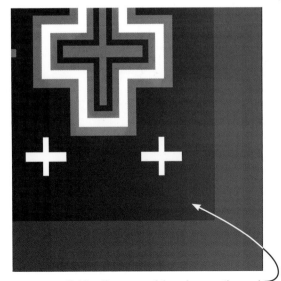

Folding the corner of the nylon over the wool

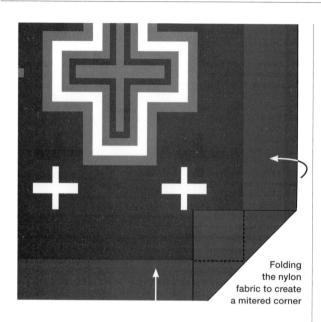

Folding
the nylon
fabric to create
a mitered corner

3. Turn the top edge of your nylon fabric down over the blanket fabric, smoothing it down. Pin in place.

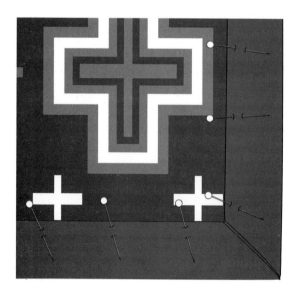

Pinning the nylon fabric and wool for topstitching

4. Repeat steps 2 and 3 on the other three sides of the blanket. Topstitch around the nylon to join the picnic blanket layers and bind the perimeter of the blanket.

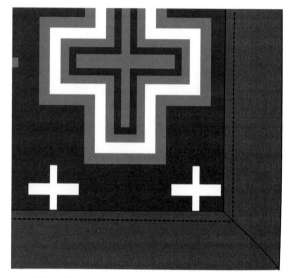

Topstitched blanket

Make the Carrier

5. Cut one 10-in. piece of webbing and set it aside. Cut the remaining 62-in. piece of webbing in half to yield two 31-in. lengths. Mark 2 in. from one end of each long piece of webbing.

Light a match, blow it out, and quickly press the head through your marked point to pierce a small hole. Let it cool and thread a buckle onto each one, passing the prong through the small hole. Secure the loose end of the webbing to the buckle with a seam, backstitching at the beginning and end to hold it.

Measure 8 in. from the buckle end of each piece and create the harness by folding an end of the 10-in. piece of webbing around each of them. Pin in place and secure each side with a box stitch.

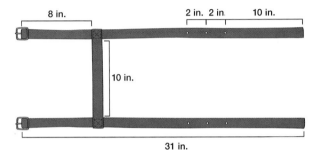

Finished harness with buckles, handle, and holes

6. Use pins to mark spots 10 in., 12 in., and 14 in. from the plain end of each webbing strap. Light a match (as you did in step 5) and use it to pierce neat, centered holes in each of those spots, making sure the two straps align.

7. Use matches or a lighter to melt the edge of the webbing in each spot so it will not fray.

Roll your picnic blanket up, place it in the webbing carrier, buckle it closed, and take it outside!

Marie Watt and Her Blanket Stories

Marie Watt, an Oregon artist who has described herself as "part cowboy and part Indian," has used Pendleton wool blankets to beautiful effect in many of her art pieces and installations. Watt, a descendant of Seneca Indians on her mother's side and Wyoming ranchers on her father's, makes intriguing work. Referencing her own life in the Pacific Northwest as well as historical and modern events, she incorporates a deep sense of community in both celebration and tragedy. In describing her *Blanket Stories* series, she wrote: "We are received in blankets, and we leave in blankets. On a wall, a blanket functions as a tapestry, but on a body it functions as a robe and a living art object.

In Native American communities, blankets are given away to honor people for being witnesses to important life events—births and comings-of-age, graduations and marriages, namings and honorings. For this reason, it is considered as great a privilege to give a blanket away as it is to receive one."

—from *Marie Watt: Lodge*; see Resources (p. 148) for more information.

Square-Within-a-Square Plaid Quilt

DIFFICULTY 🐑 🐑

TECHNIQUES Log cabin piecing (p. 14), Chain piecing (p. 17), Topstitching (p. 18), Perimeter stitching (p. 20)

I have always loved Pendleton plaids, and I wanted to make a patchwork quilt spotlighting one of my favorites, the iconic 1960s Surfer Girl Beach Boys plaid. I designed a simple log cabin quilt block to use as a center, and then made a pattern that uses 18 Pendleton fat quarters to yield a queen-size quilt, but you can make a throw or smaller size the same way using fewer fabrics. The fun part is arranging all these plaid-within-a-plaid blocks harmoniously. Plenty of rearranging and a couple dozen photos later, I was so happy with the final result. I think of it as a lake house quilt: calm, beautiful, and timeless.

FABRICS

- Pendleton shirtweight or medium-weight plaid (or men's shirting wool); I used surf plaid
- Pendleton fat quarters (or blanket-weight wool); I used 18 assorted plaids

YOU'LL NEED

- 1½ yd. of a 60-in.-wide focus shirting-weight or medium-weight plaid for centers (this is the exact amount needed, so in case of cutting error you may want to start with a little more)
- 18 Pendleton fat quarters or quarter-yards for the surrounding squares, assorted or repeating
- Wool for backing, cut to measurements of finished quilt top (shown: 80 in. by 90 in.)
- Sewing machine
- Thread
- Rotary cutter and cutting mat
- Quilting ruler
- Pins
- Paper and pen
- Steam iron

note I didn't trim selvages for this project, since you need all 60 in. of the focus fabric to yield 10 squares, and you also need to use as much of the supporting fabrics' widths as you can. Because of the ½-in. seam allowance, the selvages disappeared into my seams.

Prepare the Fabrics

1. Cut or tear your focus fabric into nine 6-in. strips that are the width of the fabric. Cut each of these strips into ten 6-in. squares for a total of 90 squares.

2. Cut or tear your supporting plaid fat quarters or quarter-yards into 3-in. strips, also the width of the fabric. If you're using fat quarters, you'll have six strips 27 in. to 30 in. long. If you're using quarter-yards, you'll have three strips 54 in. to 60 in. long. Pin all the strips together at one end so you have them handy.

Choosing Your Color Palette

This project is very customizable and could be made with a mix of plaids and solids, vintage and new fabrics, or any other configuration you like. I recommend restricting your color palette a little for overall harmony, using your focus plaid to set the tone, and collecting plaids with those colors in mind. I included plaids with all kinds of blue, green, rust, gray, brown, tan, and cream tones, avoiding strong, eye-catching colors that didn't feel like a good fit. This quilt would also be stunning in an intentionally bolder palette, different from my calm lake house tones.

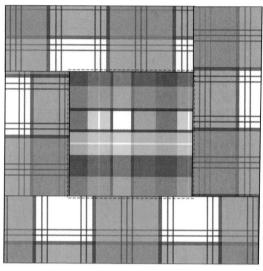

Single Square-Within-a-Square Quilt block with topstitching

Piece the Squares

3. Use the basic log cabin piecing technique (p. 14) to join strips of your first supporting plaid to five of the center squares, either piecing one strip at a time and trimming or piecing with simple chain piecing (p. 17). Piece clockwise and press your seams away from the center square.

4. Repeat step 3 to create a total of 90 blocks. This makes a very tall, satisfying stack of squares!

5. Press each block, front and back, so that the seams are pressed away from the center and lie flat. Topstitch each block, backstitching to reinforce the last stitches. Trim threads.

6. Use a rotary cutter and quilting ruler to square up your blocks so that each one has straight, even edges.

Plan the Layout

7. Now comes the most fun and challenging part. I highly recommend teaming up with a friend or a couple of friends for choosing the final layout.

Using a floor or design wall, lay out ten rows of nine blocks, trying to mix colors and plaids to draw the eye all over the quilt. Try to avoid clumps of darker or lighter similar-reading plaids in certain areas by rearranging or adjusting your layout. Take digital photos and look at those as well—an invaluable tool for planning a quilt.

8. When you are happy with your arrangement, take a final photo for reference. Write the numbers 1–9 on slips of paper and pin or staple them to the leftmost block in each row.

9. Make a neat stack of the first row, with the numbered block at the top of the pile, and work your way from left to right until you have stacked all nine blocks in the correct order.

10. Repeat step 9 for rows 2–10. You can stack these numbered-row stacks together into one large pile, but be careful not to mix up blocks!

Sew the Quilt

11. Assemble your stacks into rows: Beginning with row 1, sew your first block of the grid to the second one, using a ½-in. seam allowance. Continue sewing blocks together until all nine are joined. Press them back and front. Set this completed row aside, but do not take the numbered paper off the first block yet.

12. Repeat step 11 to assemble and press nine more rows of nine blocks.

13. Join the bottom edge of row 1 to the top edge of row 2. Pin the rows together, matching seams and pinning there. Use a ½-in. seam allowance to join them.

14. Now add the next three the same way, so you have completed rows 1–5 of the upper half of this quilt top. Set this lovely piece aside.

15. Starting with rows 6 and 7, assemble the lower half of the quilt top, completing rows 6–10 from top to bottom.

16. Working carefully, pin the bottom of row 5 to the top of row 6, matching seams. This quilt top will be very heavy, so be sure to use a chair or sewing table to support its weight. Sew these sections together to complete your quilt top. Press this final seam.

17. Measure your quilt top (mine measured 80 in. by 90 in.) and cut a piece of wool fabric the same size to use as the backing. You can also piece a backing

9 block × 10 block layout

from smaller cuts of wool. If you've used mostly light, shirting-weight plaids for the quilt top, you can use a medium- or blanket-weight backing to create a very cozy quilt.

18. Place your backing fabric on a flat surface or floor, right side up, and carefully place your quilt top over it, so right sides are together. Pin around the perimeter, leaving an opening of about three blocks along one side for turning.

19. Carefully sew the quilt top and backing together around the perimeter, leaving the opening unsewn. Clip corners and turn the quilt right side out, opening corners. Press the quilt all around the perimeter and pin it at the edges. Press the raw edges of the opening ½ in. to the inside and pin them the same way.

20. Using a neutral thread color, topstitch around the entire perimeter of the quilt, about ⅛ in. from the edge. Backstitch when you reach the beginning of your stitching to secure it.

Optional: Tie your quilt with wool or pearl cotton thread.

Improvisational Patchwork Quilt

DIFFICULTY 🐑 🐑

TECHNIQUES Topstitching (p. 18), Backing quilts (p. 20), Perimeter stitching (p. 20)

This improvisational-pieced project is very personal, drawing on your favorite fabrics and colors to create a truly one-of-a-kind quilt without using a pattern. I have collected Pendleton scraps for years, both left over from other sewing projects or found in the by-the-pound bins at the Pendleton Woolen Mill Store. I keep them in boxes sorted by solids, jacquards, and plaids. The process is intuitive; there is no wrong way to do it, and the results can be stunning.

FABRICS

- Pendleton Jacquard Blanket fabric (or mid-weight wool)
- Pendleton Blanket Fabric (or blanket-weight wool)
- Pendleton Worsted or Plaid Flannel (or light, apparel-weight wool)

YOU'LL NEED

- Assorted scraps and pieces of wool in a harmonious color palette, about 2–4 yards total
- Backing fabric, the size of your completed quilt type
- Scissors
- Sewing machine with compatible-color thread
- Rotary cutter and cutting mat
- Quilting ruler
- Pins
- Steam iron
- Digital camera

Putting Scraps to Use

Cutting up old blankets or using leftovers from other projects is a great way to build this kind of project. I mixed jacquard and blanket-weight wools of various sizes, from larger squares of about 20 in. to narrow strips, into this quilt. If you are using very lightweight fabrics as well, I'd recommend underlining them with a second layer of flannel or shirting and stitching around the perimeter to reinforce them.

The first improvisational wool quilt I ever made was this black-and-white one shown on p. 87. I designed and sewed it in memory of my father on the anniversary of his passing. The design is inspired by a geo-metric wooden cube he built in design school in the 1960s. I wanted to make something I thought he would like, and the process of pulling, arranging, and sewing these graphic, beautiful, strong colors and fabrics in memory of him was very healing. The next day was my sweet nephew's birthday, and I made the colorful warm quilt shown on the facing page using the same basic technique, with him in mind.

Make the Quilt

1. Choose one or two focus fabrics in medium or larger pieces to inspire your quilt design, using any color palette you'd like. For the black-and-white quilt, I began with a large piece of Pendleton blanket-weight wool in Condensed Black and White, about 20 in. by 24 in., and pulled lots of gray, white, and black jacquards and blanket fabrics that felt right with it. Place this focus fabric (or fabrics) down on a large, open flat space—a living-room floor is ideal.

   Lay out other complementary fabric pieces, smaller and medium sizes alike, around the focus fabric, paying attention to how your eye reads their contrast and tone. Arrange and rearrange them until you like the assortment. Take at least one photo. Don't worry if it looks busy or the fabrics are a little edgy together— they often begin to harmonize more when they are neatly stitched together without raw edges, floor, or overlaps showing.

2. When you like the design, begin joining these chosen fabrics into a column or row, trimming them to a straight edge if necessary. Sew them with a ½-in. seam allowance, pressing or folding the seam to one side. Topstitch along the seams to catch all layers. If you are unhappy with any of your choices, simply use your seam ripper to deconstruct the topstitching and joining seams of that area, take the fabrics out, and replace or rework them. Continue growing this area into a vertical column or horizontal row of a good size. This section will be the heart of your improvisational quilt. (I didn't measure any of my quilt designs as I sewed, but for reference, the heart of my quilt was approximately 24 in. wide by 40 in. high.)

3. Bring this sewn section back to your other fabrics and set it down. You may notice new patterns or relationships between fabrics, and you may want to change some of your placement and arrangements. Don't be afraid to cut fabrics into more than one piece and use them in different areas of your quilt so they echo each other.

   Just as you arranged and rearranged to create that first column, create a second one of about the same height or width, with fabric sections of any size, and sew those pieces together with topstitching.

General improvisational quilt layout for reference

4. Continue arranging, rearranging, and taking photos of your fabric layout around the heart of the quilt and its other finished sections. Try for good movement, balance, and energy. Don't be afraid to flip fabrics over to use the reverse colorway, use smaller sections as bridges between larger ones, trim pieces down to fit, or turn patterns on their sides to create contrast.

You may want to use strips to join pieced sections to one another, and to spotlight off-center parts of jacquard patterns—to me, they are just as beautiful and eye-catching as the perfectly centered, symmetrical patterns of a more traditional quilt.

5. When you have joined several pieced row or column sections, continue building in any direction. I like to add longer horizontal (width of fabric) scraps that frame the pieced center.

Continue piecing and topstitching your fabrics until you feel that the quilt design is complete. My black-and-white quilt measures 50 in. by 60 in. and uses 29 pieces total, and my colorful quilt measures 80 in. by 80 in. and uses 60 pieces total.

6. Press and trim your finished quilt top so its edges are straight. Choose a backing that complements the colors or patterns in the top, but be careful of its weight. I used almost all blanket-weight pieces in my quilts, making them heavy and substantial, so I chose very lightweight backings—a light worsted gray for my black-and-white quilt, and a rust-colored Umatilla Plaid for my warm tones quilt. Measure your top and cut your backing slightly larger.

7. Place your backing on a large, flat surface, right side up. Place the improvisational quilt over it, right side down, and pin all around the perimeter, leaving an 18-in. to 20-in. opening for turning. Stitch around the entire perimeter (except for the unpinned opening), using a ½-in. seam allowance and backstitching at the beginning and end of the seam.

8. Shake the quilt out and clip corners, then turn it right side out through the opening, gently opening the corners and smoothing the two layers together.

9. Press the perimeter of the quilt, front and back, pinning the edges as you go to keep them neat, aligned, and flat. When you reach the opening, fold and press the raw edges under ½ in. or to match the surrounding finished edges. Pin those neatly as well.

10. Using a longer stitch length, edgestitch around the perimeter to finish the quilt neatly, catching the pinned raw edges inside the seam. Backstitch to finish the seam and trim all threads. Shake your finished quilt out and let it lie flat to set the final piece so that the two layers cling to one another.

Optional: If you'd like to tie your quilt, use a curved hand needle and pearl cotton or wool yarn to tie it. Write a special label for your quilt with your name, the year you created it, your inspirations, or any other details, and hand- or machine-stitch that on the back of the quilt.

6 Go-To Accessories

Whether you sew a stylish laptop case that doubles as a clutch, a practical, graphic backpack, a beautifully detailed modern tote, or an instant-favorite messenger bag, wool is the perfect fabric for sewing sturdy and beautiful bags. Or play with pattern to make a shoulder bag's gorgeous serape stripes the star of the design!

Laptop Sleeve/Zip Clutch

DIFFICULTY 🐑 🐑 🐑

TECHNIQUES Tearing and cutting wool (p. 13), Topstitching (p. 18), Working with leather; optional (p. 23)

This simple zippered sleeve can be made to fit any laptop or e-book reader, and can even be used as an everyday clutch. The sleeve is cut a bit longer than your device, letting you slide the device in and out of the zippered opening easily.

As with any simple design, the quality shines through in the details. A panel of canvas, wool, leather, or vinyl reinforces the bottom for durability and style. A heavy metal zipper is finished with contrasting ends for a professional look. The pouch is lined for even more durability. Designed by Sarai Mitnick.

FABRICS

- Pendleton Blanket Fabric or Jacquard Fabric for the main fabric (or mid-weight to blanket-weight wool); Sarai used Condensed Black and White
- Wool, canvas, waxed canvas, leather, or vinyl for the contrast fabric
- Nylon ripstop for the lining

YOU'LL NEED

- ½ yd. wool for main fabric
- ½ yd. lining fabric
- ¼ yd. contrast fabric
- Heavy-duty metal zipper, at least 1 in. longer than your laptop
- Scissors
- Measuring tape
- Pattern paper
- Ruler
- Rotary cutter and cutting mat (optional)
- Coordinating thread
- Sewing machine with straight stitch foot and zipper foot
- Pins
- Water-soluble fabric marker
- Steam iron
- Bamboo point turner or knitting needle
- Hand-sewing needle

Measure and Cut the Fabrics

1. Using a measuring tape, measure the width of your device across the side the zipper will go on.

2. Measure the depth of the device by laying it flat on a table and measuring from the table to the highest point of the device.

3. Add the width and depth measurements, then add an additional 3¼ in. to that measurement (1¼ in. of this is for seam allowance and 2 in. is for ease and zipper tabs). This measurement will now be your total width.

4. Measure the length of the device. Add the depth and the length measurements. Add an additional 2¼ in. to this measurement (1¼ in. of this is for seam allowance and 1 in. is for ease). This measurement will now be your total length.

5. With a ruler and pattern paper, create a rectangle that measures your total width by total length. This will be your main pattern piece. Create another pattern piece that measures your total width by 5 in. This is your contrast pattern piece.

6. Using your main pattern piece, cut two large rectangles from the main fabric and two large rectangles from the lining fabric.

7. Using the contrast pattern piece, cut two rectangles from the contrast fabric.

8. Cut two 2-in. squares from the contrast fabric to form the zipper ends.

Attach the Contrast Fabric

9. On each main outer piece, mark a line 3¾ in. from the bottom.

3¾ in.

Bottom

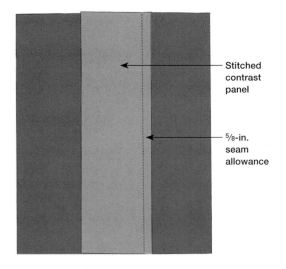

Stitched contrast panel

⅝-in. seam allowance

10. With right sides together, align the contrast panel with the line you drew. The contrast panel should be lying flat near the middle of the main outer panel. Stitch using a ⅝-in. seam allowance.

11. Fold the contrast panel down and press.

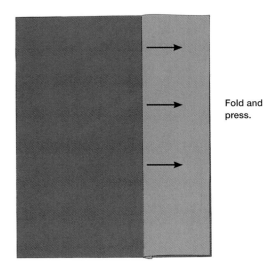

Fold and press.

12. Baste the contrast panel to the main outer panel along the remaining three sides to hold it in place.

13. Edgestitch the contrast panel along the top seam. Topstitch a second row ¼ in. from the first row.

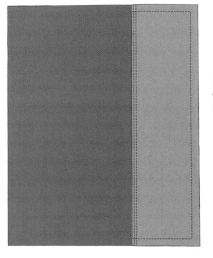

Edgestitched contrast panel

Install the Zipper

14. Trim the zipper so that it is 1½ in. shorter than the total width. You may need to cut off the zipper stops, but these will be covered again later to prevent the zipper head from coming off. In the meantime, take care not to slide the zipper head completely off the zipper.

15. Fold each of the 2-in. squares of contrast fabric in half. Then fold the raw edges toward the center and press. Your squares should now look like small lengths of binding.

16. Wrap the binding around each end of the zipper to cover and stitch in place.

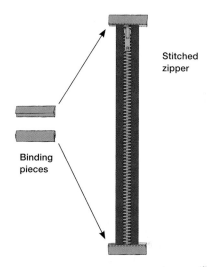

Stitched zipper

Binding pieces

17. Lay out one piece of lining, right side up. With the wrong side of the zipper facing the right side of the lining, pin to the top, centering the zipper. Baste.

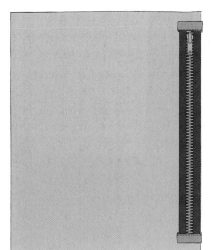

Basted zipper and lining

18. Place a main piece on top of the lining, right sides together. The zipper should now be sandwiched between the lining and main pieces.

19. Using a zipper foot, stitch through all layers along the top. When you reach the zipper head, sink your needle down into the fabric, lift the presser foot, and move the zipper head by unzipping. Lower the presser foot and continue stitching until you reach the edge.

20. Press the seam allowance toward the lining. Understitch the seam allowance to the lining. This will help prevent the lining from rolling and getting caught in the zipper.

21. Press the lining and outer panel away from the zipper.

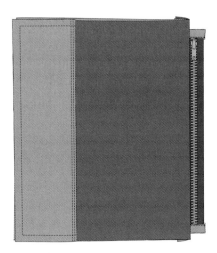

Pressed lining and panel with zipper

22. Repeat this process to sew the remaining lining and outer panels to the other side of the zipper.

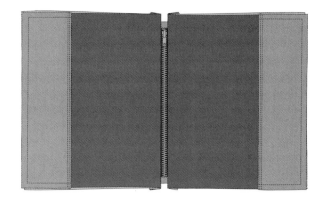

Stitched zipper with lining and outer panels

23. Open up the zipper completely. With right sides together, pin the two lining pieces together. Pin the two main fabric pieces together. Make sure seams are aligned near the zipper tabs and the contrast panel.

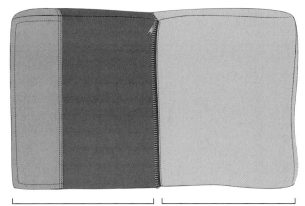

Stitched outer panels   **Lining with opening**

24. Stitch around the edges, leaving an opening at the bottom of the lining. Don't sew through the tabs, but sew close to them.

25. Clip the corners and trim the seam allowances to ¼ in. Turn the entire bag through the opening you left in the lining. Use a bamboo point turner or knitting needle to gently push out the corners. Press.

26. Slipstitch the opening in the lining closed by hand.

Jacquard Fabric Designs

Intricate woven fabric designs like the striking Condensed Black and White pattern used here are known as jacquard, after Joseph Marie Jacquard, the inventor of a brilliant mechanical addition to a standard loom that could dictate complex color patterns and designs. Jacquard's 1801 invention used punched cards to lift and lower warp threads, and was said to do the work of 100 painstaking master weavers.

The Bishop family reopened Pendleton Woolen Mills in 1909 to weave trade blankets with Jacquard looms. An Indian master weaver might spend months creating an intricate design by hand, at a rate of several inches per day, but mills could offer mass-produced blankets much more reasonably. The precious hand-woven blankets commanded higher prices, so an artisan could trade a single hand-woven blanket for a variety of mill blankets, as well as many other goods.

A Jacquard loom design had to be symmetrical (radiating out on both sides from a center point) by necessity, but a hundred years later, modern CAD (computer-aided design) looms can weave huge-scale asymmetrical or abstract patterns just as easily. However, Pendleton's fabric designers often hand-weave their fabric samples on small looms in-house before choosing final colorways to send to the mills for larger production runs—a beautiful parallel with the company's earliest days.

Jacquard Backpack

DIFFICULTY 🐑 🐑

TECHNIQUES Topstitching (p. 18), Centering designs; optional (p. 22)

What could be more useful and practical than a stylish backpack? This one uses gorgeous fabrics from Pendleton's Jacquard Blanket line in a stylish and deceptively simple design. Every piece in this project is a rectangle, so no fancy piecing is required. If you are new to lining a bag, don't worry; this lining technique is pretty easy once you get all your pieces pinned together in the right order. Designed by Heather Mann.

FABRIC

- Pendleton Jacquard Blanket Fabric (or blanket-weight wool); Heather used Rancho Arroyo in aqua
- Pendleton Eco-Wise Wool (or upholstery-weight wool)
- Pendleton Melton (or jacket-weight wool)
- Pendleton Umatilla Plaid (or 100% cotton quilting-weight) for lining
- Leather or vinyl

note I used Jacquard Blanket wool, but this project will also sew up neatly if Eco-Wise or Melton wools are used.

YOU'LL NEED

- ½ yd. wool (A)
- ½ yd. lining fabric (B)
- A piece of leather about 6 in. by 12 in. or more (C)
- Four buttons (1 in. or larger)
- Heavy-duty or leather sewing machine needle
- Sewing machine
- Pins
- Needle
- Coordinating thread
- Measuring tape
- Scissors
- Steam iron

Cut the Fabrics

1. Cut fabrics to the following dimensions.

Fabric (A):
- One 16-in. by 14-in. rectangle for front of backpack
- One 14-in. square for back of backpack
- One 3-in. by 14-in. strip for upper back of backpack
- Four 7-in. by 14-in. rectangles for flap and straps

note For the front of the backpack, see "Centering Designs" (p. 22) for tips on intentionally spotlighting a graphic section of a blanket or jacquard design.

Fabric (B):
- Two 16-in. by 14-in. rectangles for backpack lining

note Press all fabrics with a steam iron.

Fabric (C):
- Two 1½-in. by 6-in. leather strips for straps
- Two 1½-in. by 12-in. leather strips for straps

note The strap size is totally customizable. For longer straps, cut longer pieces of leather. Do not use pins to hold leather, as they will permanently puncture the leather. See p. 23 for more information on working with leather.

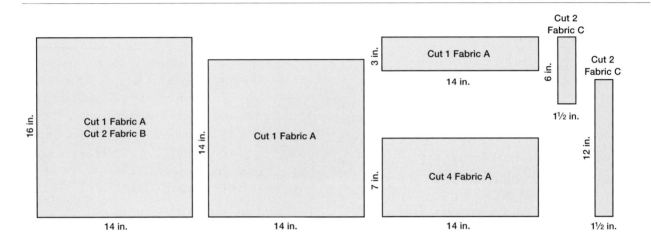

Sew the Straps and Flap

2. Use two of the 7-in. by 14-in. rectangles to make the straps. Fold one piece lengthwise, right sides facing together. Pin and sew along the 14-in. side using a ½-in. seam allowance.

3. Turn the tube so the seams are centered on one side, and iron seams open.

4. Turn the tubes right side out, making sure the seam is still centered. Fold ½-in. seam inside one end of the strap and press with your iron.

5. Insert a 1½-in. by 12-in. piece of leather into the end of the strap and pin in place. Make certain the right side of the leather is facing away from the strap's center seam.

6. Topstitch across the seam and leather sandwich, and then from the bottom of the strap up both sides of the strap. Repeat steps 2–6 for the second strap.

7. Pin two of the 7-in. by 14-in. rectangles with right sides together. Sew around the two short sides and one long side. Clip corners. Turn right side out and press with your iron.

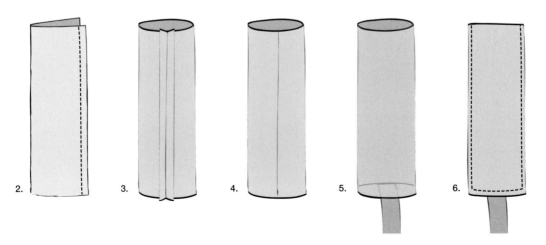

8. Place the straps along the top of the 14-in. square piece (the back of the backpack), each about 2 in. from the edge with the right side of the straps facing out. Place a 3-in. by 14-in. strip across the top of the straps with the right side facing down. Pin all the pieces together along the top. Sew across the top to secure the straps to the back of the backpack. Press the top strip open, then topstitch across the strip near the seam.

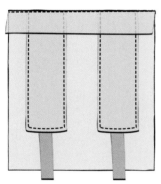

Sew the Lining and Backpack

9. Pin the right sides of the lining pieces together around the sides and bottom. Sew the sides and about 1½ in. in on each side of the bottom, leaving most of the bottom open. Turn the lining right side out.

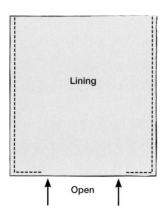

Lining

Open

10. Pin and sew the right sides of the front and back of the backpack together around the sides and bottom, making sure the straps are tucked inside and will not be caught in the seam. Clip the corners. With the backpack still inside out, pin the flap to the back side of the backpack above the straps with right sides together. Insert the lining inside the backpack, right sides together. Pin the lining to the backpack around the top opening, making sure the side seams are lined up. Sew around the top pinned area.

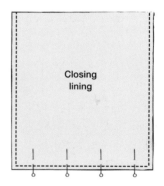

Closing lining

11. Turn the backpack by pulling the outside through the opening in the bottom of the lining piece, making sure the corners are pushed out crisply. The lining should be sticking out of the backpack. Fold the open area of the lining inside so the seam is facing inward. Pin, then sew across the bottom to close the opening. Push the lining down inside the backpack and topstitch around the top edge.

Attach the Straps and Buttons

12. Place the 1½-in. by 6-in. leather straps about 2 in. from the edges on the top of the flap. Attach the straps to the flap with a box stitch (as shown in the photo on p. 97).

13. Sew two buttons to the front of the backpack and two buttons to the back bottom. Cut a 1½-in. slit in the straps to create buttonholes. Attach the straps.

Serape Shoulder Bag

DIFFICULTY 🐑 🐑 🐑
TECHNIQUES Topstitching (p. 18), Centering designs; optional (p. 22)

The secret of this bag is in the stripes. Careful placement of the pattern and a slight tapered shape create a bold, modern statement. This bag was designed to spotlight the serape pattern, but you could use a jacquard, plaid, or solid for equally gorgeous results. Designed by Michelle Freedman.

FABRICS

- Pendleton Stripe Jacquard Blanket Fabric (or mid-weight wool) for bag; Michelle used Serape
- Pendleton Worsted (or light, apparel-weight wool) for lining

YOU'LL NEED

- 32 in. by 64 in. (two repeats of the Stripe Jacquard) for the exterior fabric (A)
- 1 yd. worsted or a lightweight woven fabric for the lining (B)
- 2 yd. of 2-in. cotton webbing for the bag straps (C)
- One 12-in. by 18-in. sheet of ultra stiff plastic canvas (such as Darice®)
- ¼ yd. of fusible interfacing
- ⅛ yd. of fusible fleece batting
- 2 magnetic snaps
- Scissors
- Measuring tape
- Quilting ruler
- Rotary cutter and cutting mat
- Thread to coordinate with fabrics (A) and (B)
- Sewing machine with presser foot and walking foot
- Pins
- Fabric marker
- Point turner
- Steam iron
- Tracing paper

Cut the Fabrics

1. Copy and enlarge your pattern for the bag and lining (pp. 135–136) on the tracing paper. Cut out the patterns. With fabric scissors, cut out one of each pattern piece of exterior fabric and lining fabric.

2. Cut the following:
   – Two 2-in. by 16-in. strips of medium-weight fusible interfacing
   – One 3-in. by 16-in. strip of fusible fleece batting
   – One 3-in. by 16-in. strip of the solid area of the stripe jacquard
   – One 3-in. by 16-in. strip of plastic canvas

note The repeat on the bag shown here is 16 in. It is measured from the centers of the solid area so the stripes are centered.

3. With the iron, follow the manufacturer's instructions to fuse the interfacing to the wrong side of the exterior bag at the top of both ends.

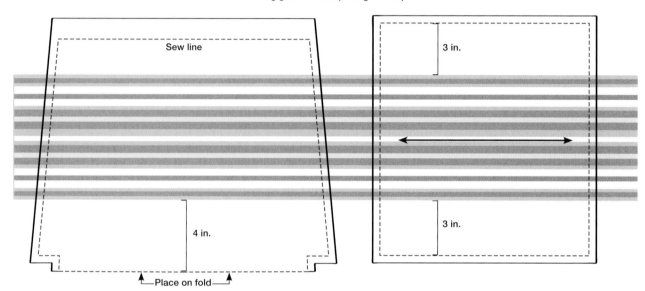

Cutting guide for serape bag and flap

Sew line

3 in.

3 in.

4 in.

Place on fold

Construct the Flap

4. Fold the short sides of the flap in half, right sides together, and pin. With your walking foot, stitch together using a 1/2-in. seam allowance, securing with a backstitch at the beginning and end of the seam. Lay the flap down with the solid areas on either side of the centered seam; the stripes will be on the outer side. Pin the raw edges together across the bottom opening and sew across to close. Clip corners. Turn the flap right side out, gently pushing out the lower corners of the flap with a point turner or pencil.

note When sewing through the thicker layers, use a heavier needle, a slightly longer stitch, and a walking foot.

5. Affix a magnetic snap to each lower corner of the underside of the flap. Follow the manufacturer's instructions to attach the snaps to the fabric.

Make the Bag Exterior

6. Press the 3-in. by 16-in. strip of fusible fleece batting to the 3-in. by 16-in. solid wool strip. Lay the strip, fleece side down, over the wrong side of the center bottom of the bag. Stitch 1/8 in. down each 16-in. side to create a reinforced bottom.

7. Fold the exterior bag in half, right sides together. Pin and baste the two long diagonal sides. With your walking foot, stitch them together, securing with a backstitch at the beginning and at the end of the seam. Press the side seams open.

   Create a box corner at the bottom of each side of the bag. Align each of the short sides with the seam allowance centered in the middle to the bottom edges. Pin the raw edges together and stitch across, securing with a backstitch at the beginning and end of the seam.

Box corner as seen from outside

Make the Lining

8. Repeat step 7 to make the bag lining, leaving a 3-in. opening on one side to turn the bag through to the right side later. Note that the lining is shorter than the exterior, which will create the facings.

9. Gently turn the exterior of the bag right side out, pushing out the lower corners of the bag with a point turner or pencil. Press the bottom edges with a steam iron. Insert the 3-in. by 16-in. strip of plastic canvas. Tack in place by hand, careful to only catch the interior layers.

Attach the Flap and Straps

10. Pin the flap to the center of the right side of the exterior of the bag and baste in place. Pin each end of one 32-in. strap to either side of the flap and baste in place. Mirror the placement of the strap on the opposite side of the exterior.

    Place the lining over the exterior bag, right sides together, and match the top raw edges and side seams. The flap and the straps should be tucked inside the bag, creating a bag sandwich. Stitch around the top edge of the bag. Turn the bag to the outside through the opening in the lining.

    Mark the position of the snaps on the exterior of the bag with a fabric marker. Attach the snaps on the exterior of the bag following the manufacturer's instructions. Hand-stitch the opening in the lining closed with a small overcast stitch.

Finish the Bag

11. Press the top of the bag to create a crisp edge. Secure all straps with a box stitch. On the back of the bag, reinforce the flap with a stitch at the top and bottom of the facings.

12. Pinch the upper corners of the bag together on each side and whipstitch them closed.

note For matching stripes in fabric (A), I suggest basting the sides together and sewing from top to bottom on both sides using a walking foot. This will prevent the fabric from slipping and keep the stripes perfectly lined up on the side seams.

Modern Embroidered Tote

DIFFICULTY 🐑 🐑 🐑
TECHNIQUES *Working with leather (p. 23)*

This tote features angled piecing with a machine-embroidery arrow accent. The design is meant to evoke traditional motifs in a stylized way, layered over gorgeous, warm colors. The embroidery is optional—either done by hand, using hand or machine appliqué, or simply omitted. The tote is fully lined and includes interior pockets, leather handles, and a magnetic snap closure. The finished size of the bag is 15 in. by 17 in., with 13-in.-long straps. Designed by Meredith Neal.

FABRICS

- Pendleton Melton (or jacket-weight wool); Meredith used Royal
- Pendleton Eco-Wise Wool (or upholstery-weight wool) for exterior; Meredith used Ivory
- Pendleton Lightweight Wool or Flannel (or men's shirting wool) for lining; Meredith used Plaid Flames.

YOU'LL NEED

- ½ yd. of wool for the contrast triangles
- ½ yd. of wool for the center diamond
- ½ yd. of lightweight wool for lining and pockets
- Pattern pieces (pp. 137–138)
- 1 yd. fusible interfacing (such as Pellon® Shape-Flex®)
- Approximately 4-in. by 15-in. piece of leather for two straps
- One magnetic snap closure
- Small piece of a heavy interfacing to reinforce snap closure
- Scissors
- Pins
- Ruler
- Steam iron
- Fabric marker
- Awl
- Clover Wonder Clips
- Sewing machine (embroidery capabilities optional)
- Coordinating polyester thread for construction
- Isacord #4103 machine embroidery thread (optional)
- Clapper

note The embroidery design shown here was purchased and downloaded from Meringue Designs (meringuedesigns.net), a wonderful collection of modern embroidery designs. Choose the file type readable by your machine. Most designs can be easily transferred from computer to sewing machine using a USB drive.

Cut the Fabrics

1. Copy and enlarge the Modern Embroidered Tote pattern on pp. 137–138. Cut the following:
   - Two each of pattern pieces (A), (B), and (C)
   - One pocket (D)
   - Two pieces of leather (E) measuring 1½ in. by 14 in.
   - Two 16-in. by 18-in. rectangles for lining

note These solid wools have no right side, so it's easy to flip them to be the appropriate side.

Embroider the Tote

2. Purchase and download the chevron stripe design from Meringue Designs in the appropriate file type for your sewing machine (meringuedesigns.net/chevron-stripes).

3. Using the placement lines on the pattern piece, hoop and stitch the design. I used the 3-in. by 7-in. design and adjusted it slightly. The finished embroidery should measure approximately 2½ in. by 6⅝ in.

Construct the Exterior

4. Join pieces (A) and (B) with right sides together. Stitch the long diagonal using a ½-in. seam allowance. Press. Notice the cut-out notch; this reduces bulk at the bottom seam by distributing it off center.

5. Join (C) along the diagonal to create one of the exterior pieces. Repeat for the back. Press the seams as you go, using lots of steam and pressing the seams open with a wood clapper. Avoid pressing down hard with your iron; you can leave iron marks on your wool.

6. With right sides together, sew exterior pieces together along the sides and bottom with a ½-in. seam allowance. Press the seams open as much as possible.

Try using a walking foot if you're having trouble moving both layers through evenly.

7. Create box corners (pp. 102–103) at the bottom of each side of the bag. Center your side seam and press over the bottom seam, lining them up to create a triangle. Sew across at the point that is 1½ in. down from the tip and 3 in. across from the seam in the middle.

8. Apply interfacing to the two lining pieces, following the manufacturer's instructions. This can be a time-consuming process, but one well worth doing. Always work from the center out and resist moving your iron from side to side. Lift and lay the iron to prevent the interfacing from stretching out.

Construct the Pocket and Lining

9. Fold the top edge of the pocket ½ in. toward the wrong side, then fold 1 in. toward the right side. Stitch through all layers along the sides and along the single layer of the bottom using a ½-in. seam allowance. Turn the top pocket edge 1 in. toward the right side and press. Edgestitch the fold down. Press the sides and bottom of the pocket along the stitch line you created.

tip

Use a thread mark to help with pressing so that you can press along your stitch line instead of measuring.

10. Place the pocket approx. 3 in. down from the lining's raw edge, lining up the plaid so the pocket looks seamless. Edgestitch around the sides and bottom, joining the pocket to the lining. Reinforce the top pocket corners with an extra line of stitching.

11. Follow the manufacturer's instructions to add the magnetic snap closure 1½ in. from the top raw edge of each lining piece, ensuring it will only go through the lining and not be seen on the exterior.

12. Place the right sides of the lining together. Sew the sides and bottom edge with a ½-in. seam allowance, only sewing about 2 in. on each side of the bottom of the bag to leave an opening for turning. Backstitch at each edge of the opening. Trim threads.

13. Press open the seam allowance. Box corners as you did for the exterior.

Sew and Attach the Straps

14. Fold each strap with wrong sides together. Beginning 2 in. above the end of the strap, stitch along the raw edge, pivot across the handle, then stitch back again along the folded edge, pivoting again to stitch a complete rectangle around the strap.

15. Place the end of the handles flush with the top edge of the outer bag (which should be facing right side out), 8 in. apart. There should be 4 in. on either side of the center. Because of bulk, try clipping the pieces together instead of pinning. With the wrong side of the lining facing out, slip the outer bag with handles inside the lining, matching side seams. Sew around the top edge with a ½-in. seam allowance. Reinforce the handles by sewing a second seam, anchoring them to the seam allowance. Trim as close to the wool as possible at the side seams at the top edge to reduce bulk. Turn the bag right side out through the opening in the bottom seam of the lining.

16. Press the top seam flat, with the lining lying over the seam allowance. Take the time to edgestitch your lining ⅛ in. from the seam allowance to help your lining stay inside the bag.

17. Edgestitch the opening at the bottom lining seam closed. Place the lining inside the bag and press the top edge with a lot of steam so the lining falls inside. Use the clapper with steam to set the bulky fold at the side seams.

School Days Messenger Bag

DIFFICULTY 🐑 🐑 🐑

TECHNIQUES Topstitching (p. 18), Centering designs; optional (p. 22)

This wool messenger bag is inspired by vintage school bags and satchels. With magnetic snaps and wool trim, this bag is slightly more challenging to sew, but the result is worth the effort. The bag is fully lined and has one flat, interior pocket. On the flap of the bag, you can feature a centered motif like the striking Mini Chief Joseph to really highlight the beauty of Pendleton jacquard. Designed by Alexia Marcelle Abegg.

FABRICS

- Pendleton Jacquard Blanket Fabric (or blanket-weight wool) for main bag; Alexia used Mini Chief Joseph
- Pendleton Melton (or jacket-weight wool) for contrast; black
- Quilting-weight cotton fabric or cotton flannel fabric for lining

YOU'LL NEED

- 1 yd. jacquard fabric for main bag (this allows enough fabric to center the motif for the bag front flap)
- ½ yd. melton for bag contrast and strap
- Messenger Bag patterns (p. 139)
- 1 yd. lining fabric
- 1⅜ yd. 20-in.-wide woven fusible interfacing, such as Pellon Shape-Flex
- Two ⅝-in. magnetic snaps
- Scissors
- Ruler
- Thread to match or coordinate with main fabric and contrast fabric

- Sewing machine with presser foot
- Pins
- Fabric chalk marker
- Steam iron
- Press cloth
- Rotary cutter, rotary cutting ruler, and cutting mat (optional)

note Seam allowance throughout: ⅜ in.

Ironing Tips

Use a 14-in.-square press cloth cut from muslin between the iron's surface and the face of the wool fabric when pressing and ironing or fusing interfacing to the wool. This cloth helps protect the face side of the fabric from the iron and keeps the fabric from getting iron shine, an impression left from using an iron directly on the wool fabric.

Cut the Fabrics

1. Cut the following pieces, enlarging the patterns as needed.

Main bag fabric:
– Two pieces 2½ in. by 13 in. for bag bottom
– Two pieces 12 in. by 2½ in. for bag sides
– Two pieces 12 in. by 13 in. for main bag front and back
– One Flap Panel pattern piece (p. 139)

Contrast fabric:
– One piece 3⅞ in. by 55 in. for bag strap
– Four Tab pattern pieces (p. 139)
– Two Snap Square pattern pieces (p. 139)
– One Flap Contrast pattern piece (p. 139)

Interfacing:
– One piece 2½ in. by 13 in. for bag bottom
– Two pieces 12 in. by 2½ in. for bag sides
– Two pieces 12 in. by 13 in. for main bag front and back
– One Flap Panel pattern piece (p. 139)

Lining:
– One piece 2½ in. by 13 in. for lining bottom
– Two pieces 12 in. by 2½ in. for lining sides
– Two pieces 12 in. by 13 in. for main lining front and back
– One piece 9 in. tall by 13 in. wide for bag pocket
– One Flap Panel pattern piece (p. 139)

note Cut bag pieces to measurements listed by using a rotary cutter, rotary cutting ruler, and mat, or by drafting measurements onto the wrong side of your fabric with chalk and ruler, and cutting with scissors.

Press all pieces with a steam iron. Fuse interfacing to the wrong side of the corresponding main bag pieces following the interfacing manufacturer's instructions.

Construct the Main Bag

2. Place the flap contrast on the main flap piece with the wrong side of the contrast touching the right side of the flap panel. Topstitch the contrast to the flap panel ⅛ in. from the inside raw edge.

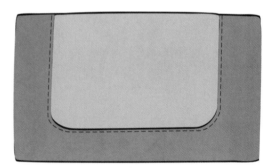

Flap with contrast

3. Sew the flap lining to the flap right sides together along the sides and lower edge using a ⅜-in. seam allowance. Trim the lower corners to eliminate bulk. Turn right side out and press. Topstitch the seam ⅛ in. from the sides and lower finished edges.

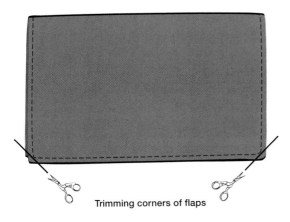

Trimming corners of flaps

4. Install the male side of one magnetic snap on one tab piece at the marking indicated on the tab pattern piece. Repeat with the male side of the remaining magnetic snap and tab piece.

5. Sew one plain tab piece to one tab piece with a magnetic snap installed with the wrong sides together by topstitching the two pieces together $\frac{1}{8}$ in. from the cut edges. Repeat with the remaining tab pieces.

Tab with snap

6. Following the placement guide on the pattern piece, topstitch the upper edge of the tab pieces to the bag flap by stitching a $\frac{3}{8}$-in.-by-width-of-the-tab rectangle at the upper edge of each tab.

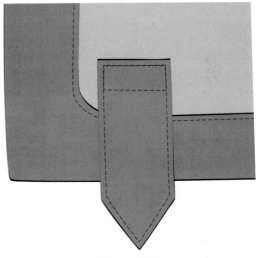

Tab sewn to flap

7. Following the placement guide on the pattern piece, install the female side of each magnetic snap to each of the snap square pieces.

8. Topstitch the snap squares with snaps installed to the front of the main bag panel front, centering each square $3\frac{1}{2}$ in. from the side edges and $2\frac{1}{8}$ in. from the lower edges.

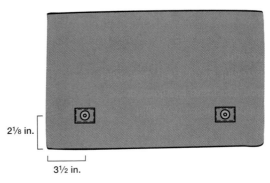

$2\frac{1}{8}$ in.

$3\frac{1}{2}$ in.

Snap placement

9. Sew the main bag panel front to the side of one main bag side piece with the fabric right sides together. Start at the upper edge and sew toward the bottom, stopping ⅜ in. from the lower edge and backstitching.

Bag panel front and side

10. Continue constructing the bag in the same way as in step 9, placing fabric right sides together, starting at the upper edge and sewing toward the bottom, then stopping ⅜ in. from the lower edge and backstitching. Construct the pieces in the following order:

Sew the main bag panel front to the side of the remaining bag side piece.

Sew the main bag panel back to the remaining long side of the side piece sewn in step 8.

11. Sew one long side of the bag bottom panel to the main bag panel front. Start sewing ⅜ in. from the corner of the bag bottom panel, stopping ⅜ in. from the opposite corner and backstitching. Repeat with the remaining long side of the bag bottom panel and the main bag panel back.

12. Sew one short side of the bag bottom panel to one main bag side panel. Start sewing ⅜ in. from the corner of the bag bottom panel, stopping ⅜ in. from the opposite corner and backstitching. Repeat with the remaining short side of the bag bottom panel and the main bag panel back.

13. Press a ¾-in. hem along the upper edge of the pocket piece and topstitch. Place the pocket wrong side onto the right side of one of the main bag lining pieces, aligning the lower and side raw edges. Pin.

Pocket with hem

Construct the Lining

14. Sew the bag lining in the same fashion as the main bag pieces, following steps 6–11. When sewing the bag lining bottom seam, leave a 6-in. opening centered in one of the bag bottom seams for turning the bag right side out.

Attach the Straps

15. Fold the strap piece lengthwise with right sides together and sew the long raw edges together with a ³⁄₈-in. seam allowance. Turn the strap right side out and press flat with the seam centered on the back of the strap. Turn ½ in. to the inside at each short end of the strap and topstitch the strap ⅛ in. from the edges all the way around.

   Optional: Topstitch the strap once again, stitching ³⁄₈ in. to the inside of the previous topstitching all the way around.

16. Place the short finished ends of the strap 2½ in. below the upper raw edge of the bag sides. Topstitch the strap ends to the side panels of the main outer bag, stitching a rectangle 1 in. tall and the width of the strap.

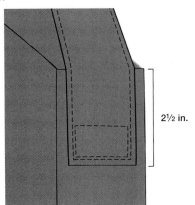

2½ in.

Strap sewn to bag

Finish the Bag

17. Pin the bag flap right sides together to the main bag panel back. Fold the bag strap down toward the bottom of the bag. This will keep the strap out of the way for the stitching in the following step.

18. Place the main bag inside the bag lining with the right sides together and pin the upper edges together all the way around. Sew the bag upper edge seam in one continuous stitching line all the way around the upper edge of the bag.

Bag tucked inside lining

19. Pull the bag right sides out through the opening in the lining. Sew the opening in the lining seam closed by hand or by machine.

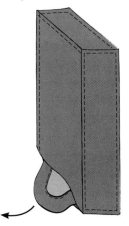

Lining inside bag

20. Push the lining to the inside of the bag and press the upper, finished edge of the bag.

7 Favorites to Wear

Soft, warm wool is perfect for sewing special things to wear—a scarf that's as cozy as it is beautiful, a striking draped shawl, a sleek and elegant obi belt, or a stunning hooded winter cape edged with smooth felt. Sew any of these projects as a gift, or keep them for yourself, in your favorite colors and patterns.

Fitted Scarf

DIFFICULTY 🐑
TECHNIQUES Running stitch (p. 18), Topstitching (p. 18)

This soft and feminine wool scarf is lined with silk and closes with an oversize decorative button. It's perfect for the first chilly days when you really don't need a heavy coat or jacket—just a little something stylish and cozy to keep you warm.

FABRIC

- Pendleton Merino (or soft, mid-weight wool); I used one plaid and one houndstooth

YOU'LL NEED

- One fat quarter of soft wool
- Fitted scarf pattern (p. 140)
- 18-in. by 30-in. piece of lining-weight silk in a complementary color
- Coordinating thread
- Contrasting thread, for basting
- One oversize sew-in snap (U.S. size 10)
- One large decorative sew-through button or large covered button kit
- Steam iron
- Pressing cloth
- Pins
- Hand-sewing needle and thread
- Scissors
- Microtex sewing machine needle
- Sewing machine
- Seam ripper

Make the Scarf

1. Carefully press the silk fabric with a low-heat iron and no steam under a pressing cloth. Press the wool fabric, after adjusting your iron temperature setting to "wool" and steam, again using a pressing cloth.

    Copy and enlarge the scarf pattern (p. 140) to the wool along a fold and cut it out. Pin the pattern to the silk the same way and cut it out carefully.

    Using a needle and thread in a contrasting color, hand-baste the fabrics, wrong sides together, around the perimeter with long running stitches (p. 18), ¼ in. from the edge. Don't bother to knot your basting stitches; you'll want to be able to remove them easily after you machine-sew. Leave a 4-in. to 5-in. opening unbasted along the inside of the curve for turning right side out later.

2. Starting at one end of the unbasted section, use the Microtex needle to machine-stitch the silk and wool fabrics together with a ¼-in. seam allowance. Stop at the other end of the 5-in. opening. Be sure to backstitch at the beginning and end of the seam.

3. Remove all hand-basting stitches with a seam ripper or scissors. Clip the curves and turn the scarf and lining right sides out, gently pushing out the ends with something like a chopstick.

4. Press the scarf on a low/medium setting using a pressing cloth. Carefully press the raw edges of the opening under ¼ in. Pin the opening together. Topstitch or edgestitch around the perimeter of the scarf, including the opening, backstitching at the beginning and end of the seam to secure.

5. Try on your scarf and mark where it overlaps comfortably. Stitch one half of a large snap to the bottom layer of the scarf at that spot on the wool side. Stitch the other half of the snap to the top layer at that corresponding spot on the silk side. Hand-stitch a large decorative button over the snap, or make a large covered button following package directions and hand-stitch that on.

Men's Scarf

DIFFICULTY 🐑

TECHNIQUES Felting (p. 23), Blanket stitch (p. 19)

I made this reversible scarf as a present for my husband, Andrew. I felted the wool fabrics at home, brought them along on our summer vacation, and blanket-stitched the scarf from start to finish on a road trip through Eastern Oregon—a perfect way to pass the time driving through such a beautiful place. This is a wonderfully simple project, but the fabrics you choose make it your own. I paired one of my favorite jacquard patterns, Harding, with a striking contrast menswear plaid that picked up some of the same beautiful colors while offering its own distinct statement.

FABRICS
- Pendleton Lightweight Jacquard Blanket Fabric (or mid-weight wool); I used Harding
- Pendleton Shirtweight Plaid (or men's shirting wool)

YOU'LL NEED
- ¼ yd. each of two fabrics of your choice
- DMC #642 pearl cotton thread
- Scissors
- Needle
- Pins (optional)

note The scarf size is variable: I made this one 7 in. wide and let the width of the fabric (60 in.) dictate the length of the scarf.

Make the Scarf

1. Lightly felt the two quarter-yards of fabric if you'd like to make the texture a little more cozy and soft. I felted both my jacquard and plaid fabrics by washing them twice and then drying them (see p. 23 for more details on this process). If you prefer a lightweight, crisper scarf, skip this step.

2. Tear or cut the fabrics so that they're exactly the same width (I made mine 7 in., but you can make yours narrower or wider), and trim the pieces to the same length. I left selvages on my fabrics, but you can trim yours away if you'd prefer.

3. Align the two fabrics, wrong sides together, pinning if you'd like. My fabrics clung to each other nicely, so I didn't need to pin them in place.

4. Thread a needle with pearl cotton thread and blanket-stitch the two fabrics together along all four sides. Finish with a secure knot and bury it between the two layers.

Stylish Shawl

DIFFICULTY 🐑

TECHNIQUES Decorative stitches (p. 121)

This project is a sophisticated blanket-inspired shawl that you can layer over anything before heading out of the house. A lighter-weight fabric will offer more drape, and a heavier-weight wool will give more structure and change the feel of the shawl. Either would work nicely. This quick project offers a great outerwear option that can be layered and really showcases beautiful fabric prints. Designed by Lupine Swanson.

FABRICS

- Lightweight to medium-weight Pendleton Jacquard Blanket Fabric (or mid-weight wool); Lupine used a PORTLAND COLLECTION lightweight jacquard

YOU'LL NEED

- ½ yd. wool
- Scissors
- Sewing machine with coordinating or contrast thread
- Dritz® Wash Away Wonder Tape or pins for basting

note This shawl would also look great made from plaid, flannel, or any other patterned wool.

Make the Shawl

1. Using scraps of fabric, bits of wool, or felt, test a variety of stitches on your sewing machine. Choose your favorite stitch and practice it on your test scrap.

2. Lay out fabric and create a rectangle 18 in. by 60 in. This is a half-yard measurement right off a bolt. Do not trim selvages.

3. Lay out your fabric so that one of the short ends meets the opposite side of the fabric along one long edge. This forms a cone shape of fabric, with a longer length to one side. The top is the smaller opening, and the bottom opening remains wide and asymmetrical (as seen on p. 120).

4. Overlap the short edge of the fabric by ¼ in. Hold in place using Wash Away Wonder Tape or pins.

5. Starting at the top, stitch along the basted section, being sure to secure the top part of the stitches well. Take your time.

6. *Optional:* Trim the front triangle to a gentle curve. If you'd like to use the same or a more discreet decorative stitch on the top and bottom openings, add that now. Otherwise, leave the wool unfinished.

tip

Use an open-toe embroidery foot for step 6 if you have it. It creates great visibility for stitching.

note The wool used here needed no edge finishing, so the top neckline and bottom edge were left raw. If you would like to finish the edges by hand, a blanket stitch would also work well to close the edge and could be done along the top and bottom openings as well.

7. Trim thread tails, slip the shawl over your head, and strike a pose! This shawl can be worn with a gentle folded edge if you'd like to show a contrast in fabric weaves. Have fun; only you know you are essentially wearing a blanket in public!

Decorative Stitches

This project utilizes decorative stitches found on most modern sewing machines. You could use a variety of lovely stitches to join along the only seam and add either a pop of color and style, or an understated, stylish closure. If your machine is without much besides a zigzag stitch, just play around with that using a wide stitch width and short stitch length to achieve a simple, smooth satin stitch. I used a stitch that had width and a smooth geometric look and feel in a thread color that matched the fabric.

Obi Belt

DIFFICULTY 🐑 🐑
TECHNIQUES Topstitching (p. 18)

This striking obi belt uses the mini version of Pendleton's iconic Chief Joseph pattern, lined with black worsted wool, but you can choose any two light- or medium-weight jacquard, plaid, or solid wool fabrics you like for this project. The obi belt's same-size contrast lining also means it's fully reversible. Designed by Cally McVay.

FABRICS
- Lightweight or medium-weight Pendleton Jacquard Blanket Fabric, (or mid-weight wool); Cally used Mini Chief Joseph

YOU'LL NEED
- ½ yd. of lightweight jacquard or solid wool
- ½ yd. of contrast wool for lining
- Obi Belt pattern (p. 141)
- Thread
- Scissors
- Pins
- Sewing machine
- Steam iron
- Pattern paper

note Cally used a 14-in.-wide section of each fabric, but you may want extra for spotlighting a pattern or design.

Cut the Fabrics

1. Copy and enlarge both Obi Belt pattern pieces on p. 140 for the center and the sash. Place the Obi Center pattern on the fold of the main fabric, centering any design you'd like. Pin in place and cut it out.

2. Copy and enlarge the Sash pattern (p. 141) and cut out two pieces in the main fabric.

3. Repeat steps 1 and 2 to cut out the same sections of the lining fabric.

Sew the Obi Belt

4. Using a ½-in. seam allowance, sew one side of the obi center and the obi sash together at the widest point, aligning pattern marks. Repeat for the opposite side.

5. Repeat step 4 with the lining fabric sections. Press the main fabric and lining fabric sections.

6. Align the outer and lining obi belt sections, right sides together, and pin the pieces together all the way around the center and sash, leaving one short end of the sash unpinned.

7. Sew all the way around the belt, leaving one end of the sash open and backstitching at the beginning and end of the seam.

8. Turn the belt right side out and press the fabric on each side so it lies neat and flat.

9. Press, turn, and pin the small open section of the sash, folding the fabric inside so that there is a crisp, clean edge. Sew along the edge, closing the seam.

10. Sew the sash end of the belt on the opposite side the same way, ensuring both closed seams look exactly the same.

Winter Cape

DIFFICULTY 🐑 🐑 🐑

TECHNIQUES Topstitching (p. 18), Wool binding (p. 71, step 3)

A feminine winter wardrobe is perfectly topped with this classic hooded cape. Nothing evokes drama and elegance quite like a cape! Inspired by vintage Pendleton capes of the 1950s, this project is simple to sew. Added techniques like topstitched seams and a bound edge are lovely finishing details. And because it's an easy, one-size-fits-most fit, this cape will become a staple in your cold-weather wardrobe. Designed by Alexia Marcelle Abegg.

FABRICS:

- Pendleton Jacquard Blanket Fabric (or blanket-weight wool); Alexia used Four Directions
- Pendleton Melton (or jacket-weight wool)

YOU'LL NEED

- 2¼ yd. wool fabric for cape and hood
- 7¾ yd. wool felt binding
- Winter Cape patterns (pp. 142–143)
- One large covered hook and eye, sometimes called fur hook and eye or coat hook and eye
- Scissors
- Measuring tape
- Thread to match or coordinate with main cape fabric and binding
- Sewing machine with presser foot
- Pins
- Fabric chalk marker
- Steam iron
- Press cloth

Cut the Fabrics

1. Copy and enlarge the Hood pattern (p. 142). Using the pattern, cut two pieces with fabric right sides together.

2. Cut one piece using the Cape pattern (p. 143) with fabric folded right sides together, selvage to selvage, and folded again lengthwise. Cut out the neck opening according to the pattern. Cut down the center front line.

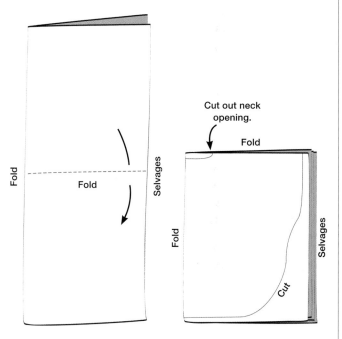

3. If your fabric is too thick to cut out when folded twice, trace the pattern onto the fabric with the fabric folded only selvage to selvage. Trace half the pattern at a time: First trace the back up to the neck opening, then flip the pattern along the shoulder foldline and trace the front of the cape. Cut on the marked line.

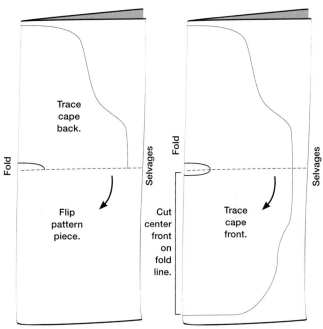

4. Press all pieces with a steam iron.

5. Pin the two hood pieces right sides together and sew the hood back curved seam using a ½-in. seam allowance.

6. Press the seam open and finish seams separately with a zigzag or serger stitch. Topstitch the pressed-open seam ¼ in. to the left and right of the seam.

Press Cloth

Use a 14-in. square cut from muslin or silk organza as a press cloth between the iron's surface and the face of the wool fabric when pressing and ironing. This cloth helps protect the face side of the fabric from the iron and keeps the fabric from getting iron shine, an impression left from using an iron directly on the wool fabric.

7. Pin the hood neck edge to the neck opening of the cape piece with fabric right sides together, and match the notches at the center back and center front edges. Sew the neckline with a ½-in. seam allowance. Press the seam toward the hood and finish the seam with a zigzag or serger stitch. Topstitch seam ¼ in. from the seamline through the hood fabric and seam allowances.

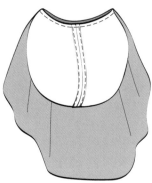

8. Fold the entire piece of felt binding in half lengthwise. Press.

Fold and press.

9. Bind the continuous outer edge of the cape and hood beginning at the center-back lower edge of the cape. Stitch the binding ⅛ in. from the cut edge, enclosing the raw edge of the cape in the binding. When you get to the center-back lower edge, stop stitching 5 in. before you reach the beginning binding edge.

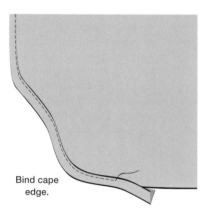

Bind cape edge.

10. Trim the binding end so that the ends overlap by ½ in. Finish binding the remaining 5 in., again overlapping the binding ends. Unlike a blanket project, you don't need to add a second row of stitching.

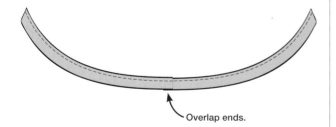

Overlap ends.

11. Sew the covered hook and eye to the inside of the front neck opening of the cape.

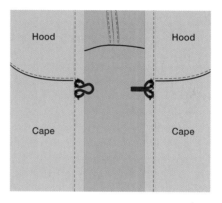

Hood   Hood

Cape   Cape

12. Fold the cape armhole opening wrong sides together on the shoulder foldline and tack the cape, front and back together, through all the layers following the marking on the pattern piece as a guide.

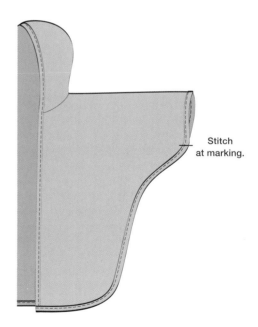

Stitch at marking.

Appendices/Patterns

Here are all the patterns that you'll need for the projects in this book, plus resources for finding fabrics, caring for wool, and further sewing adventures! You'll also find a timeline of Pendleton's fascinating history, including lots of images from their vast corporate archives.

Cut 1 at 100% to use as template.

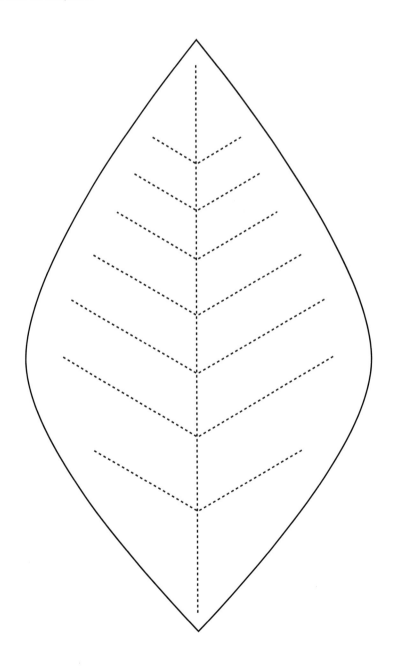

Cut 1 at 100% to use as template.

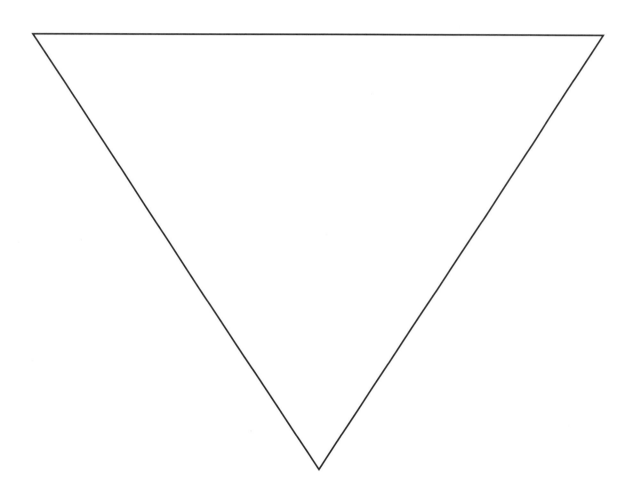

PLANTER BASE

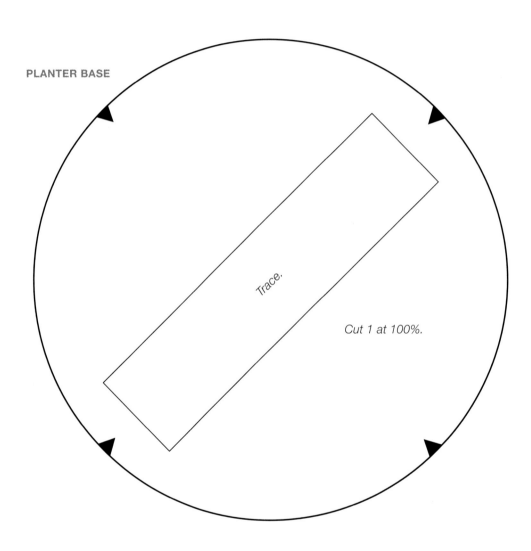

Trace.

Cut 1 at 100%.

PLANTER BASE GUIDE

Cut 1 at 100%.

PLANTER SIDE

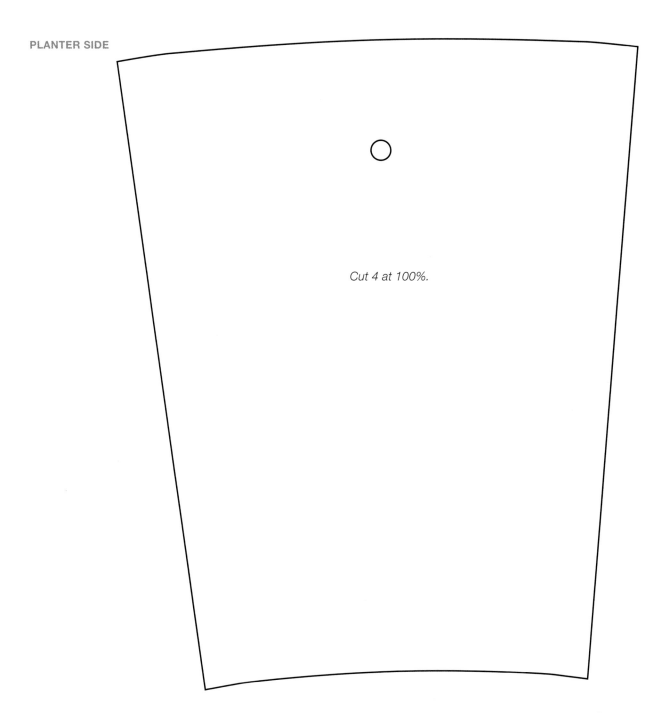

Cut 4 at 100%.

Cut 1 at 100%.

CHEVRON PILLOW

Enlarge 333%.

FABRIC A EXTERIOR

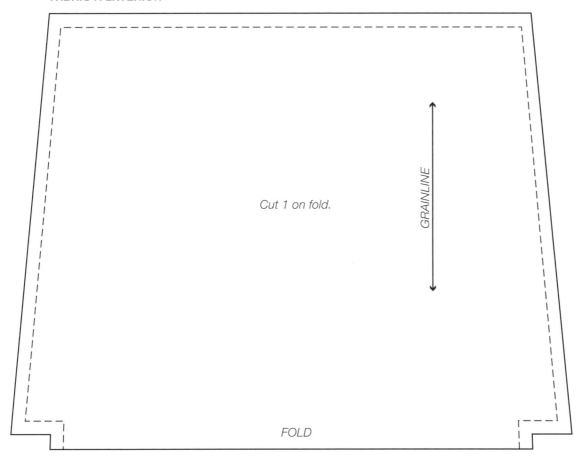

Cut 1 on fold.

GRAINLINE

FOLD

Enlarge 333%.

FABRIC A FLAP

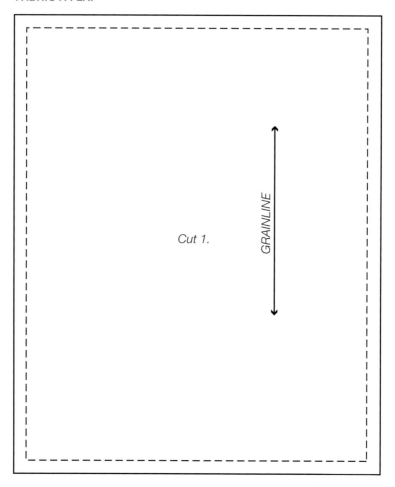

Cut 1.

GRAINLINE

Enlarge 333%.

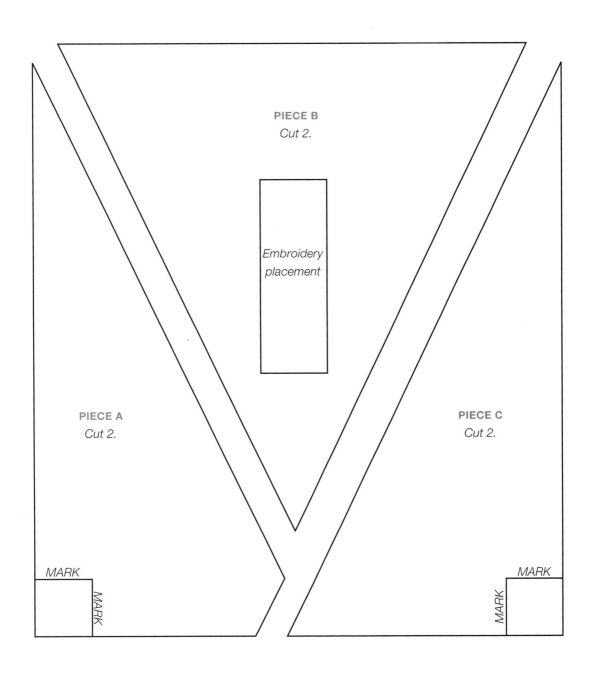

Enlarge 333%.

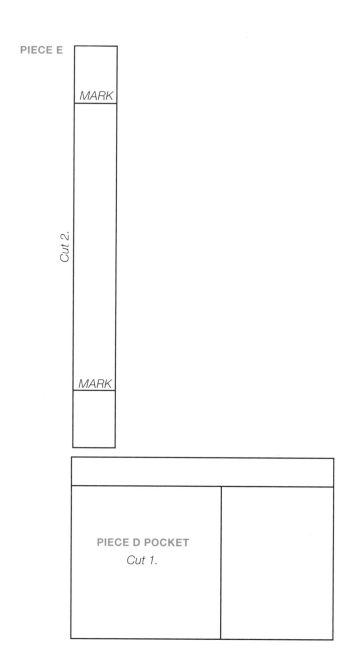

PIECE E

MARK

Cut 2.

MARK

PIECE D POCKET

Cut 1.

Enlarge 200%.

FLAP PANEL

Cut 1 on fold.

Wool Jacquard

Tab Placement

FOLD

FLAP CONTRAST

Cut 1 on fold.

Contrast

FOLD

TAB

Cut 4.

Contrast

SNAP SQUARE

Cut 2.
Contrast

Enlarge 200%.

COLLAR

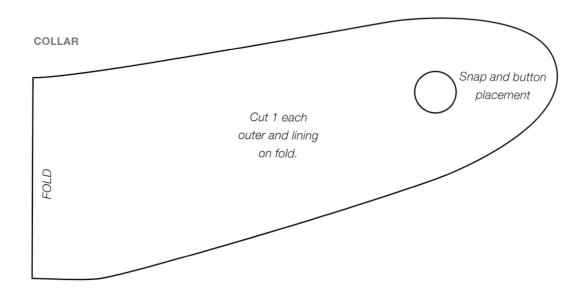

Snap and button placement

Cut 1 each outer and lining on fold.

FOLD

Enlarge 333%.

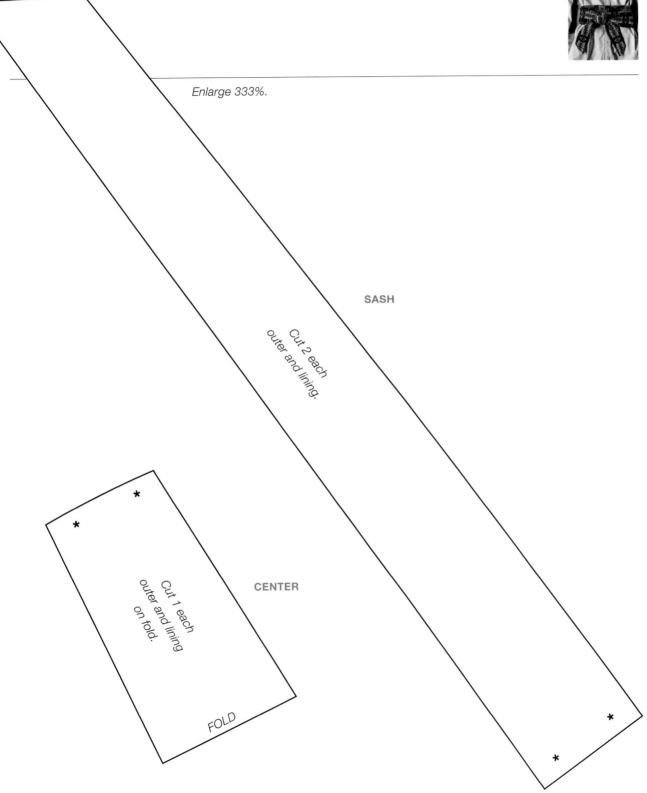

SASH

Cut 2 each
outer and lining.

CENTER

Cut 1 each
outer and lining
on fold.

FOLD

Enlarge 400%.

HOOD

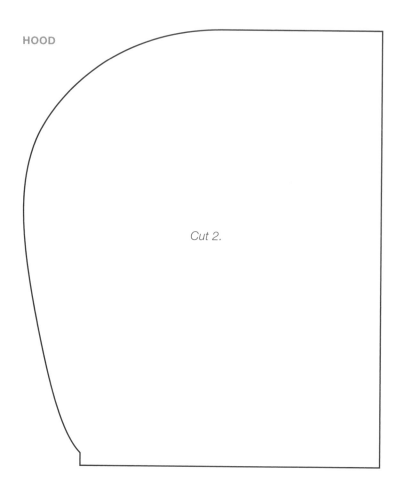

Cut 2.

Enlarge 400%.

FRONT/BACK

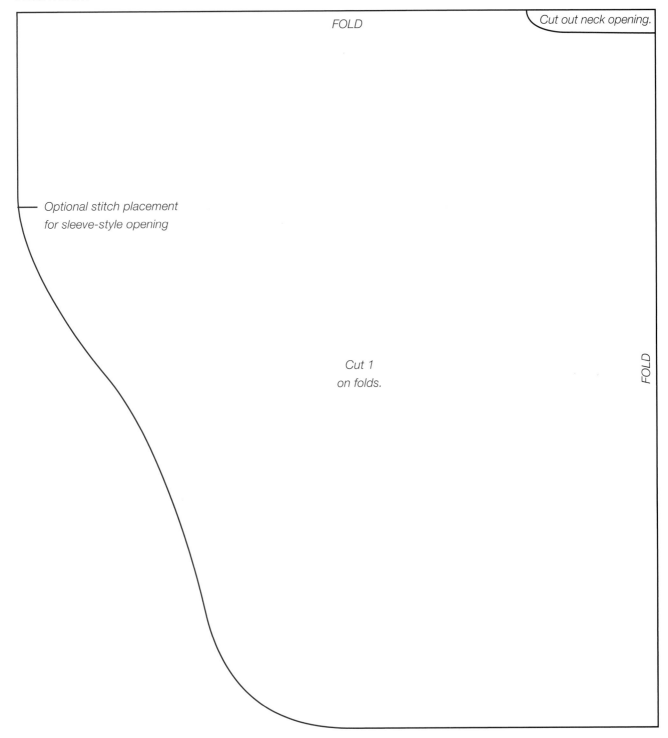

FOLD

Cut out neck opening.

— Optional stitch placement
for sleeve-style opening

Cut 1
on folds.

FOLD

Pendleton Timeline

Pendleton Woolen Mills is famous for its beautiful blankets, fabrics, and clothing. Woven into the tradition and quality instantly recognizable in each of their fabrics is a remarkable streak of innovation, tenacity, and risk taking. In many ways the story of Pendleton mirrors the history of America itself, through the vivid decades of economic booms and busts, wars and peacetimes. The vintage and new goods bearing the "Warranted to be a Pendleton" label have a special resonance today as ever, and owe their inspiration to a young immigrant who struck out on his own risky path to build relationships and respectful bonds with the Indian customers who influenced his company's most iconic blanket designs.

The company's beginnings reach back thousands of miles and over 150 years. Take a look at the timeline starting above right to see just how Pendleton came to be Pendleton!

1860: Ann and Fannie join Thomas by emigrating to the U.S.; a year later, the mill he worked for burns down.

1863: Thomas is recruited for a new woolen mill planned to be built and operated in Oregon; he arrives in the tiny town of Brownsville after an arduous journey by sea, crossing the Isthmus of Panama by burro. For the next two decades, Thomas manages and oversees woolen mills in Western and Southern Oregon.

1909: Fannie and C.P. Bishop, at the behest of the citizens of Pendleton, Oregon, invest in the Pendleton Woolen Mill and assume ownership, trademark, and goodwill of the company, building a brand-new factory on the south bank of the Umatilla River. "Sheep to Shawl" manufacturing operations officially began on September 1, 1909, with a line of Indian trade blankets of "the highest degree of perfection in manufacture," with the finest and purest colorings," using the "finest Oregon fleece wool" designed by Joe Rawnsley, who traveled to live with Western Indian tribes to learn what designs were of special cultural significance. The fledgling mill's first and most important customers were the Cayuse, Walla Walla, and Umatilla Indians who lived nearby. Pendleton designed and wove colorful trade blankets for them to use as important ceremonial gifts, marking births, celebrations, rituals, and funerals.

All images found within the timeline have been provided courtesy of Pendleton Woolen Mills.

1837: Thomas Lister Kay born in West Yorkshire, England, and at the age of nine begins work as "bobbin boy" at a mill in Shipley, in an era with no child labor laws and no protections for workers. By age twelve, he becomes a spinner's apprentice, then spends the next few years learning the weaving trade.

1857: Thomas Kay marries fellow Yorkshire native Ann Shipley, and following the birth of their daughter Fannie, leaves England for New York in search of work. The Industrial Revolution had brought a wave of fresh opportunities to America, and hundreds of new textile mills were at the forefront. These mills offered the possibilities of huge profits, but were also vulnerable to devastating losses, particularly from fires, and volatile markets. Thomas Kay spends the next few years working in mills in New York, Pennsylvania, and New Jersey, ultimately becoming foreman of a 21-loom operation.

1889: Thomas opens his namesake company, The Thomas Kay Woolen Mill, in the state capital of Salem. The Kay family by now numbered ten children. Thomas Kay's oldest daughter, Fannie, was his closest confidant; he never learned to read, so Fannie's day-to-day assistance in family business matters was essential. Fannie married a merchant and businessman named C. P. Bishop, who expanded the original Kay family enterprise to include a wholesale shop in Portland, among other endeavors. Thomas passes away in 1900. His three Bishop grandsons, Clarence (also known as C. M.), Roy, and Chauncey, continue to learn every aspect of the family textile business.

Early 1900s: The original Pendleton Woolen Mill in Eastern Oregon, which produced popular, colorful round-cornered Indian trade blankets, falters and closes, hampered by tariffs, absentee owners, a leaking roof, and outdated equipment.

continued on p. 146

In January 1910, a group of Eastern bankers visited the Pendleton mill on a brief tour of the city. Twenty-eight men, including co-owner C. M. Bishop, stood on the mill dock, robed in Pendleton Indian trade blankets, in a stunning impromptu portrait of the early mill days. The bankers, impressed with the operation, bought nearly a hundred blankets before leaving on the Union Pacific Railroad. The mill's workers also posed with the blankets they were proud to card, dye, spin, and weave the wool for, in a similarly beautiful portrait of this era (at left).

continued from p. 145

1912: Pendleton purchases the former Union Woolen Mill in Washougal, Washington, to accommodate the company's growth. During the war years, the company diversified into manufacturing military fabrics and blankets, then men's shirts, coats, and other garments, all of the highest quality virgin wool.

Longtime dyer Lester Kiser kept careful records of decades' worth of hundreds of the company's blankets' designs and colors, including this special adaptation of the first blanket in the National Parks series, Glacier National Park, into a coat design. His meticulous handwritten notations and color shadings show how much care and detail went into every aspect of the fabrics and blankets alike, whether it was for a custom order, a new garment design, or a catalog blanket. At the time, there were hundreds of jacquard blanket designs in the Pendleton line.

1923: President and Mrs. Harding visit Oregon to dedicate the Old Oregon Trail at a ceremony that draws 30,000 people. The Cayuse tribe presents the First Lady with one of Pendleton's blankets, specially created for the occasion, in a smaller size ideal for wearing as a robe or shawl. The design, known as the Harding, became wildly popular and is still in the line today.

1949: As post-war life for many Americans returned to normal, with new time for leisure activities like camping and hunting, the company noticed something interesting: many of its wholesale re-orders from shops included a disproportionate number of extra-small and small men's shirts. It became clear that women were buying and wearing these colorful plaid shirts as lightweight camp jackets, so in 1949 the company launched its first womenswear: the 49er, a simple, unlined plaid jacket with mother-of-pearl buttons and bias patch pockets. Much like the colorful men's plaid shirts two decades earlier, the 49er was an immediate and iconic hit.

Early 1950s: Pendleton establishes an Old West-styled general store in the Frontierland section of the Disneyland amusement park at the invitation of Walt Disney. The Pendleton shop, which sold a full line of their garments, blankets, and dry goods, received well over a million visitors in its first year alone, and the Bishop family received a personal thank-you note from Walt Disney for their good faith in embarking on the collaboration (which is still neatly filed in the company archives).

2000s: When Pendleton's head of fabric design Marsha Hahn looked back at the iconic Beach Boys album cover, forty years after it topped the charts, she was inspired to revive the original plaid pattern of their board shirts from the archives. New designer Winthur Simpliner spent her first days on the job weaving samples of this perennially appealing plaid in more than a dozen different colorways for the designers to review. Three of these were chosen to formally return to the line, including the original charcoal and blue plaid from the shirts, which also became part of a major collaboration with Vans and Hurley. You can see this same beautiful Surf design, in the red colorway, in every center of the Square-Within-a-Square Plaid Quilt blocks (p. 80).

For THE PORTLAND COLLECTION, another fashion-forward venture, Pendleton invited a trio of local independent designers to create a contemporary collection in-house, using some of the most venerable jacquards and plaids drawn from the company archives, with all garments made in the United States.

1924: Pendleton introduces their first colorful plaid wool shirts for men, which became an instant success in a market previously dominated by dull grays and browns. Quality was also paramount: a single men's shirt could use between 28 and 36 individual pieces, with all plaids matched precisely at the collar points, fronts, and pockets.

1932: Pendleton supplies the 1932 Los Angeles Olympics with 4,000 blankets for all of the games' participants, delivered from Oregon by rail car.

Early 1940s: Pendleton turns its attention to the war effort, weaving military blankets and fabrics, and awards President Truman a jacquard blanket after the war ends.

Early 1960s: In California, surfers began wearing Pendleton wool plaid shirts in the cold Pacific Ocean water (much like an early wetsuit), creating a powerful connection between fashion and surf culture. The Beach Boys (formerly known as the Pendletones) wear matching Pendleton board shirts on two of their album covers, creating intense demand for the garment.

Late 1980s: Pendleton releases its first retail catalog to keep current with new shopping trends, a departure from its previous wholesale-only business model. Instead of focusing solely on the trade blankets and heirloom-quality virgin wool garments it had always been known for, the company also continued diversifying and expanding its men's, women's, and home lines, later opening a signature flagship home store on the street level of its Portland, Oregon, world headquarters.

1990: Pendleton begins its American Indian College Fund Blankets line, which raises money for the American Indian College Fund (AICF). The series continues today, and Pendleton also designed a special blanket to commemorate the momentous opening of the Museum of the American Indian in Washington, DC.

Today: You can visit many of the Pendleton mills in person—the 1912 Washougal mill in Washington, which primarily weaves garment fabrics, and the original 1909 Pendleton mill in Eastern Oregon weaving blankets. The former 1939 Milwaukie mill (just south of Portland) has been transformed into the retail-only Woolen Mill Store. The 1889 Thomas Kay Woolen Mill in Salem is now open to the public as a museum, the Willamette Heritage Center.

Resources

Pendleton Fabric and Supplies

Pendleton sells its beautiful wool fabric directly at their Portland, Oregon, Woolen Mill Store. You can find yardage right off the roll, as well as wool scraps or smaller pieces of fabric by the pound or in bulk. One of the most popular scrap fabrics is blanket header, which refers to the fabric woven at the beginning and end of a large roll, so the loom can start and end without impacting a design. These are often the width of the bolt (up to 60 in.) and range in height, so they're perfect for piecing quilts or other patchwork projects. Despite the name, some header is much lighter weight than blanket.

Visit the Woolen Mill Store in person for a treasure hunt in its huge wooden bins. If you're not local to Portland, you can also order online or over the phone. The Woolen Mill Store blog even posts a Truck Report every week to let customers know what's arrived from the mills.

Pendleton Woolen Mill Store

8500 SE McLoughlin Boulevard
Portland, OR 97222
503-535-5786
thewoolenmillstore.blogspot.com
Pendleton-usa.com

Online Stores

eBay.com
etsy.com
Search eBay and etsy for vintage Pendleton clothing, blankets, and fabric, as well as vintage stores, thrift stores, and estate sales.

Pendleton Mills

Visit either of Pendleton's working mills for free guided tours during the week, as well as a large selection of blankets, fabrics, and other goods.

Pendleton Blanket Mill

1307 SE Court Place, Pendleton, OR 97801
541-276-6911

Washougal Weaving Mill

2 Pendleton Way, Washougal, WA 98671
360-835-1118

Books

More about Wool

All About Wool by Julie Parker (Rain City, 1996)

Wool, the World's Comforter by W. D. Darby (New York Dry Goods Economist, 1922)

Trade Blankets and History

Chasing Rainbows by Barry Friedman (Bulfinch, 2003)

Language of the Robe by Robert W. Kapoun (Gibbs Smith, 1992)

Sewing and Quilting

Modern Log Cabin Quilting by Susan Beal (Potter Craft, 2011)

Quilting Modern by Katie Pedersen and Jacquie Gering (Interweave, 2012)

Sewing for all Seasons by Susan Beal (Chronicle, 2013)

The Colette Sewing Handbook by Sarai Mitnick (Krause, 2011)

Inspiration

Marie Watt: Lodge by Rebecca J. Dobkins (Ford Museum of Art, 2012)

Online Resources

burdastyle.com
Sewing webinars, patterns, and more

coletterie.com
Contributor Sarai Mitnick's blog

creativebug.com
Wool sewing and quilting classes

reallyhandmade.com
Contributor Amy Alan's blog

Caring for Wool

Here are a few tips for caring for your precious handmade wool projects:

- Wool fabric repels dirt and dust naturally, so first gently brush away any marks you see, following the grainline of the fabric. Spot-clean any smaller spots or stains, blotting carefully with a soft white cloth. A damp sponge may also help, always blotting rather than rubbing.

- To hand-wash a garment or project, use lukewarm water and a very gentle detergent. Do not wring or twist, but wash and rinse it carefully and then gently squeeze excess water away. Let it dry between two absorbent cotton towels, lying flat or in place. Do not hang to dry.

- Some wool fabric, like men's shirting flannel or merino, is specially designed to be machine washable. Use a gentle detergent on casual or gentle setting and do not machine-dry. Pendleton generally recommends dry-cleaning wool blankets.

- Store clean wool garments or accessories in airtight containers to protect them from moths.

Find many more suggestions for caring for wool, including Wool . . . A Natural, a free downloadable brochure, on Pendleton's website at Pendleton-usa.com.

Metric Equivalents

One inch equals approximately 2.54 centimeters. To convert inches to centimeters, multiply the figure in inches by 2.54 and round off to the nearest half centimeter, or use the chart below, whose figures are rounded off (1 centimeter equals 10 millimeters).

1/8 in. = 3 mm		4 in. = 10 cm		16 in. = 40.5 cm	
1/4 in. = 6 mm		5 in. = 12.5 cm		18 in. = 45.5 cm	
3/8 in. = 1 cm		6 in. = 15 cm		20 in. = 51 cm	
1/2 in. = 1.3 cm		7 in. = 18 cm		21 in. = 53.5 cm	
5/8 in. = 1.5 cm		8 in. = 20.5 cm		22 in. = 56 cm	
3/4 in. = 2 cm		9 in. = 23 cm		24 in. = 61 cm	
7/8 in. = 2.2 cm		10 in. = 25.5 cm		25 in. = 63.5 cm	
1 in. = 2.5 cm		12 in. = 30.5 cm		36 in. = 92 cm	
2 in. = 5 cm		14 in. = 35.5 cm		45 in. = 114.5 cm	
3 in. = 7.5 cm		15 in. = 38 cm		60 in. = 152 cm	

Contributors

Alexia Marcelle Abegg

Alexia Marcelle Abegg studied fashion and fine arts in college. After trying her hand at photography, production, acting, costuming, hair and makeup for film and television, fashion design, and custom sewing, she began creating fine art quilts and sewing patterns while living in Brooklyn, New York, and working at The City Quilter. Alexia and her husband, artist and fabric designer Rob Bancroft, now live in Nashville. She currently divides her time among creating patterns for their company, Green Bee Design and Patterns; teaching; making art; designing fabric for Cotton + Steel; and writing.

Amy Alan

Amy Alan began her love affair with sewing and crafting as a young girl. She graduated with a degree in apparel design and became a patternmaker for a show apparel company. She then worked in alterations and started her own business altering wedding gowns and sewing custom quilts. She now lives in Portland, Oregon, where she runs a successful sewing blog (reallyhandmade.com) and teaches classes both in person and online.

Amber Corcoran

Amber Corcoran lives in Denver, Colorado, where she co-owns Fancy Tiger Crafts (fancytigercrafts.com), a magical shop for knitting, sewing, quilting, and hand-spinning supplies and classes. She has designed and published sewing and knitting patterns through Fancy Tiger Crafts. A graduate of Savannah College of Art and Design, she has a background in photography and graphic design, but has been focused on her passion for textiles since she learned to knit in 2002.

Michelle Freedman

Michelle Freedman is an Oregon-based designer and author with a passion for making quilts. Her work has been featured in *Stitch*, *Generation Q Magazine*, *McCall's Quick Quilts*, and other magazines. Michelle served as the 2013 president of the Portland Modern Quilt Guild and holds a BFA from Parsons School of Design. She also embroidered the Brave Star Pendleton blanket that President Obama gave to Nelson Mandela. Read more about her work on her blog, designcamppdx .blogspot.com.

Diane Gilleland

Diane Gilleland is a craft writer and designer based in Portland, Oregon. Her blog, craftypod.com, is about all things stitchy, and she's never met a craft she didn't like. She's the author of *Kanzashi in Bloom* and co-author of *Quilting Happiness*.

Sandie Holtman

Sandie Holtman has been crafting and sewing most of her life. A native of Seattle, Washington, she and her husband, Jon, raised two terrific children and are delighted first-time grandparents to Madie Jean. Sandie blogs about her quilting and knitting adventures at Sleepy Owl Studio (sleepyowlstudio.wordpress.com).

Anna Joyce

Anna Joyce is a textile and surface designer based in Portland, Oregon. Anna designs a line of hand-printed accessories for wardrobe and home and teaches modern appliqué techniques at Modern Domestic in Portland and Purl Soho in New York City. You can find more of her work at annajoycedesign.com.

Heather Mann

Heather Mann is the founder of dollarstorecrafts.com and specializes in transforming inexpensive materials into stylish and simple craft projects. She has appeared on the *Martha Stewart Show* and in *Reader's Digest*. She has also been featured in *The New York Times*. Her site was nominated for a Bloggie award in 2013.

Cally McVay

Cally McVay is a crafter by nature who loves to create and has been sewing since her mom taught her on her old Kenmore sewing machine. She recently dove back into sewing and opened her own Etsy shop, TandHWoolDesigns. She also teaches, designs projects, and works at the Pendleton Woolen Mill Store.

Sarai Mitnick

Sarai Mitnick is the author of *The Colette Sewing Handbook* and founder of indie favorite sewing pattern company, Colette Patterns. With a background in User Experience and design, Sarai is dedicated to creating patterns that teach while helping create classic wardrobe staples. Sarai runs the popular Colette sewing blog at coletterie.com, along with a free weekly sewing tips newsletter, Snippets. Visit her at colettepatterns.com to find all of this, plus free patterns, tutorials, and more.

Meredith Neal

Meredith Neal is a designer and teacher at Modern Domestic in Portland, Oregon, whose work has been featured in national Bernina promotions. Before she came to Portland, Meredith earned an MFA in Costume Design from Ohio University and worked as a costume designer in New York. You can find her embroidering more at meredithneal.com.

Haley Pierson-Cox

Haley Pierson-Cox is a craft writer and project designer based in Brooklyn, New York. She works primarily with fabric and fiber and specializes in creating beautiful, made-to-be-used, modern items. Haley blogs about her adventures in DIY at The Zen of Making (thezenofmaking .com), and is also a staff writer at *CRAFT* magazine and a co-host of Craft Social, a monthly craft-centered Twitter chat.

Stacy Spaulding

Stacy Spaulding has worked for the Pendleton Woolen Mill Store since 2006 as a teacher, eBay store manager, and creative consultant in the fabric department. Stacy also teaches sewing and crafting classes all over Portland and is the mother of three teenagers. In another life, Stacy could have been a rodeo princess—when she's not sewing, she loves to ride horses.

Lupine Swanson

As one of the proud owners of Modern Domestic in Portland, Oregon, Lupine Swanson is lucky to be around people that sew each day. She loves to put great projects together with quality tools, teach classes at the shop, and help people fall in love with sewing and Bernina machines. She lives in Portland with her husband, two daughters, and multiple sewing machines!

Index

ABOUT THE AUTHOR

Susan Beal is a craft writer in Portland, Oregon, who teaches and designs projects for the Pendleton Woolen Mill Store. She is the author of seven craft books, including *Bead Simple, Button It Up, Modern Log Cabin Quilting,* and *Sewing for all Seasons.* She's also a contributing editor at *Stitch* magazine, the historian for the Modern Quilt Guild, and the mother of two children, Pearl and Everett. See more of Susan's work, and her Pendleton projects, on her blog, westcoastcrafty.com.

If you like this book, you'll love *Threads*.